THE · MODERN
IDENTITY
CHANGER

*How to Create a
New Identity for
Privacy and
Personal
Freedom*

Sheldon Charrett

The Modern Identity Changer:
  How to Create and Use a New Identity
  for Privacy and Personal Freedom
by Sheldon Charrett

Copyright © 1997 by Sheldon Charrett

ISBN 0-87364-946-X
Printed in the United States of America

Published by Paladin Press, a division of
Paladin Enterprises, Inc., P.O. Box 1307,
Boulder, Colorado 80306, USA.
(303) 443-7250

Direct inquiries and/or orders to the above address.

Warning

Certain passages in this book may reference laws in an informal and general manner. The publisher, author, and distributors of this book do not purport to be attorneys, nor do they advocate illegal activity. The information presented in this book should not be relied upon or used without first consulting an attorney and researching the applicable laws of the appropriate jurisdictions.

Some or all of the ideas presented herein may be considered illegal in many jurisdictions of the United States and elsewhere. This book is presented *for academic study only*.

Contents

Preface

There is a movement growing within the powers-that-be to stop books such as this from being published. Our legislators propose to narrow and qualify the First Amendment to the Constitution of the United States of America to suit their desire for control. This same movement believes that the United States should enact legislation mandating a national identity card as yet another means to track, keep tabs on, and otherwise invade the privacy of the citizens of our nation.

The current interpretation of the First Amendment allows any citizen of the United States of America to legally say, "I am John Doe," "I am Ghandi," or "I am God."

We, the people, intend to keep it that way.

Acknowledgments

I wish to thank:

P.M.C., for her literary expertise, guidance, support, and unwavering belief in my nonconventionality.

R.R., for his invaluable assistance with the finer points of the Social Security Administration.

J.F., for his editorial support, kind words, and occasional bump in the right direction.

P.L., Paladin Press, and the First Amendment to the Constitution of the United States of America, for giving this book a home.

Introduction

⌣•

There is a silent, ongoing battle between the Bureaucratic Machine and those who oppose it. In their quest for privacy and personal freedom, free thinkers like identity changers are continuously exploiting loopholes in the system. In its quest to control the public, the system is continuously filling these loopholes.

One could argue that publishing books such as this only aid bureaucrats in finding the loopholes and filling them. Though this argument may have a solid basis in reality, what would the proposed solution be? To not publish?

Big Government and Corporate America need to be faced head-on. This is how battles are fought. Identity changers find loopholes by familiarizing themselves with public policy and procedure. Bureaucrats fill loopholes by studying the habits of the individuals who exploit them. The battle is, as it should be, ongoing. Thus, while you are reading this book, you may rest assured the feds are reading it too.

Rest assured? Yes, rest assured. Knowledge *is* power. Knowing that you are involved in a battle is very important. You do not want to use the information in this book with the attitude that you are "beating the system." Such an attitude could lead to trouble. This book does not teach you how to beat the system but how to *play along* with it and, hopefully, stay one step ahead of it. After you realize just where you stand, you will have a big advantage over the bureaucracies in that you can

1

react to information much faster than can they. Government is too big. This is your advantage.

THE NEED FOR UPDATED SOLUTIONS

We recognize the battle and government's need to fill all loopholes. Therefore it stands to reason that identity changers must keep pace with updated solutions.

Familiarizing yourself with such classics as *Paper Trip I & II* and other landmark books on the subject of identity changing is important and may also be of some benefit. Relying on these texts, however, is not recommended. Generally speaking, the serious identity changer should not rely on outdated materials. Published information that has been in the hands of government for more than a few years is likely to be obsolete. Although it is a sluggish bureaucracy, two years is more than enough time for the government and its various bureaus to recognize loopholes and fill them.

Clearly then, there is a need for updated solutions to the problem of identity changing. This book provides some solutions. Other recently published books on the subject of identity changing should also be consulted on a regular basis in order to keep one step ahead of the system.

PROBLEMS WITH PAST THINKING

Again, the basic problem with past thinking on identity changing is that it is no longer up to date. A technique, theory, legal loophole, or statement of law may no longer be accurate if it is learned from an old text. Some examples of past thinking that can lead a person into trouble are:

- The "infant death" method of procuring birth certificates
- Forged baptismal certificates
- Inventing Social Security Numbers
- The use of mail drops

INTRODUCTION

Though all of these examples will be explored in this book, I will elaborate a bit here on the use of mail drops to illustrate my point.

It is easy to find published directories of U.S. mail drops that purportedly offer confidential mailing addresses for the purpose of achieving personal and financial privacy. The implication is that if a person were to acquire such a directory and take advantage of a listed mail drop, then personal and financial privacy would be attained.

Nothing could be further from the truth. As you will learn in Chapter 8, major credit bureaus maintain databases of known mail drops, which are routinely compared to credit applications and existing credit profiles. If your address matches one in the database, your credit report may be flagged for potential fraud. In fact, using published mail drops could lead an otherwise unsuspecting investigator right to your door.

Is this to say that one should not use mail drops? No. The trick is to know which ones to use—certainly not one that has been published in a directory, where the credit bureaucrats can get their sticky little fingers on it. If one were to purchase such a directory, it should be for the purpose of making sure a mail drop is *not* listed in it. So if you have a mail drop directory, it may still come in handy, although not in the manner you might have guessed.

This is just one example. The sad truth is that most books on the subject of identity changing are replete with poor advice. The same can be said of most books on counterfeit identification. One book contained the following suggestion for producing a counterfeit ID. It advised the reader to procure a huge poster board about four feet high by six feet long, then, using press-apply lettering, reproduce his or her state driver's license. When this was complete, the book recommended setting up a camera and snapping a picture of yourself standing in front of the "ID." I believe that I actually became embarrassed while reading this.

• ⟶

SUGGESTED READING

Regardless of the pitfalls with past thinking, a historical study of any subject is generally a good idea, and that tenet holds especially true for the subject of identity changing in America. If you're serious about following the suggestions in this book, then follow the first one: read these books!

- *New ID in America* by Anonymous (Boulder, CO: Paladin Press, 1983)
- *Reborn in the U.S.A.* by Trent Sands (Port Townsend, WA: Loompanics Unlimited, 1991)
- *Credit: The Cutting Edge* by Scott French (Boulder, CO: Paladin Press, 1988)
- *How to Beat the Credit Bureaus* by Bob Hammond (Boulder, CO: Paladin Press, 1990)

Suggestion number two is to, at some point, read the chapters of this book in order. When they get a new book, many folks like to skip around through the chapters and browse their favorite topics first. So go ahead and get it out of your system. Just remember to go back at some point and read this book cover to cover. If a chapter is of particular interest to you, you are probably doing yourself a disservice by skipping ahead to it and ignoring the other chapters altogether.

All of the chapters in this book are interrelated. The material from one often references material in another. Thus, by reading the chapters in sequence, you will begin to see how all of the various facets of identity changing are interconnected. Then, if you decide to take that big step and actually follow the suggestions in this book, the cross-referencing among the various chapters will help guide you through your battle plan.

HOW IS THIS BOOK DIFFERENT?

This book focuses on the major pitfalls of traditional iden-

4

INTRODUCTION

tity changing while enumerating and illustrating current solutions to the problem. It is not a slim handbook on acquiring a deceased infant's birth certificate. It is the real thing, complete with step-by-step instructions and illustrations on how to properly go about acquiring a new identity, how to produce and manufacture the documents necessary to support that identity, and how to obtain credit, employment, and banking privileges for that identity.

Although some of the material in this book may prove to be useful around the world, it is assumed that the reader is primarily concerned with identity changing in the United States.

This book does not spend a lot of time covering material that has been covered in other well-known books on the subject of identity changing. For this reason, it is assumed that you are familiar with most of the old ideas. For those who are not, the old ideas generally can be derived from the context of the situations and examples presented herein.

By studying past texts and keeping current with new ones, identity changers, freedom seekers, and privacy enthusiasts can maintain a fresh arsenal of information in the war against totalitarianism. We can then look our enemies confidently in the eye. We've said that Big Government and Corporate America need to be faced head-on, and this is how battles are fought. In the coming chapters, you will learn that, in fact, this is how battles are won.

CHAPTER ONE

What Is Identity?

Webster's New World Dictionary, Third College Edition, defines identity as:

- the condition or fact of being the same or exactly alike; sameness; oneness
- the condition or fact of being a specific person or thing; individuality
- the condition of being the same as a person or thing described or claimed

Expanding on these three distinct definitions, we can demonstrate how society feels about identity. Different facets of society have different attitudes about identity. Exploring these attitudes will result in a more fundamental understanding of what identity is. You will then have a better foundation from which to employ the material outlined in the chapters that follow.

The first part of this definition describes how government feels about identity. Government pulls its soldiers, police officers, bureaucrats, and taxpayers from a group of controlled, unquestioning people. The government affectionately refers to these people as "the masses." Certainly it is advantageous for government to view the masses as having a uniform identity. It is also advantageous for government if the masses view *themselves* as having one uniform identity. For example, the U.S. government is much more likely to enlist an "American" into the armed services than a recently married individual with newborn twins, a loving family, and a self-defined philosophy of life.

Government proliferates its concept of identity by touting police officers and military personnel as model citizens. Soldiers and cops who are injured in the line of duty become instant heroes. They are awarded medals of honor, given nice write-ups in the newspapers, and are often made the feature story on television news programs when nothing else is going on in the world. They are given nice disability pensions, and they spend their remaining years telling war stories as they unwittingly advertise government's position on identity.

The second part of *Webster's* definition describes people who *do not* fall victim to the attitude of the masses. These people are true individuals. They comprise the sector of society that thinks for itself. They are philosophers, artists, entrepreneurs, and people concerned with taking responsibility for their own existence.

This definition of identity describes who a person truly is. It is our self. It is who we were as a child, that same person we struggled with as a teenager, and, hopefully, the one we become as an adult. The unfortunate plight of the individual is that too many of us stray from ourselves once formal education is completed and the reality of survival in an economic society begins.

Throughout his trip through the government-sponsored school system, the student is taught that there is a very specific paradigm that must be followed in order to "survive" or "make it" in the world. The recommended program emphasizes (and even enforces if you try to educate your children in an unapproved fashion) many years of schooling, which will yield a certain understanding of society and the physical universe. Upon completion of education, one must find stable employment to support a lifestyle. Social interaction with the opposite sex is strongly promoted, and the expectation is to be married before age 30 and "settled down" with children in your own home shortly thereafter.

If this isn't enough to keep the masses busy, competition between members of society is continually promoted to ensure perpetuation of the rat race. Certainly, if Mr. Jones has a Saab 900, then Mr. Smith next door must purchase a BMW. If Mr. Smith sends his children to Harvard, then Mr. Jones must send his children to Oxford. The result is a society full of people obsessed with social status and having too many possessions that they never have time to enjoy.

Our identity, therefore, is reduced to our career and our rank in a material society. We dismiss that child we were as we grew up in exchange for the promise of social security, safety, and a few thousand dollars a year. In short, we accept the governmental definition of identity and live out a quasi-comfortable life of conformity and predictability.

Your quest to reestablish a relationship with your true identity has led you to this book. This statement may seem odd for a book written about changing your identity. Hopefully, though, you now see that it is the government's definition of identity that we wish to manipulate in order to preserve, or in some cases rediscover, our true identity.

Webster's third definition of identity, "the condition of being the same as a person or thing described or claimed," is the definition with which the balance of this book is concerned. We will learn to supply the bureaucrats with all their little papers, stamps, cards, and tracking numbers so that they leave us alone and instead hound some person who doesn't exist. In this way, we can be who we really are and do it on our own terms whenever we damn well please. When we need something from society, we simply present them with the appropriate documents and get whatever it is we need (e.g., employment, bank account, driver's license, Social Security, etc.). If they start to hound our "identity" too much, we simply change it. The system will then be sending mail and inquiries to an unresponsive void while the identity changer peacefully goes about his or her business.

Some may inquire, "Why not just stick with the identity I've had since birth?" If you can pull it off, that's great. My suspicion is, though, that if you're reading this book, you've already realized the overwhelming amount of information that the government has pertaining to the identity with which you were born.

The government starts tracking you from the moment you are born. It knows what time you were born, where you were born, how you were born, the name of your mother and father, the birthplace of your mother and father, the name of the doctor that delivered you, and whether you were premature, late, or right on time.

When you were enrolled in school, the government started tracking your family's income, your medical history, your learning ability, your IQ, and your ability to conform. Remember those boxes on your report card? Interacts well with other children. Does what he/she is told. Keeps his/her desk in clean condition. Organizes work material efficiently. *Everything* is documented.

When you became a teenager, chances are that you were still too naive to know any better and, like most of us, willingly gave the government any information they wanted so you could drive a car or get a college scholarship. Perhaps you even thought about joining the army when you graduated from high school. Some of us actually did join the army. After all, we were trained 180 days a year to pledge our allegiance to the flag, and we were encouraged to join Cub Scouts or Girl Scouts and make our way through the ranks. If we were good enough, worthy enough, and loved our country enough, we became Eagle Scouts. We never bothered to stop and think about the words "scout" or "rank" or even "eagle." Sound like military terms, don't they?

There are other facets of your life that invariably become intertwined with your identity. Where you are geographically situated is thought by many, especially marketing types, to be a large part of who you are. Whether you buy into such things or not, "social status" or your alleged "class" are thought to be determining factors as to the type of person you are. Where you work, what type of work you do, the type of car you drive, what kind of jacket you wear, and whether or not you play bridge on the weekend are contributing determinants of your identity, as far as society is concerned.

The government desires to keep track of us in order to keep us in its system. If we should begin to get ideas of our own, we are offered a high-paying position in the government and promised a pension when we retire. Most people jump at this "opportunity" and are unwittingly swept into the system, regardless of their strong initiative and thinking ability. The perks are hard to resist.

Some of us have had run-ins with the law. Don't feel bad if this has happened to you. Enforcement of the law is one of government's favorite ways of keeping you down and busting your self-esteem and sense of self-worth. Granted, we can't go around slapping murderers on the wrist and telling rapists to exercise self-control. Clearly, there is a need for laws in any society. It is the *abuse* of the legal system to which I refer. For example, cops love to chase teenagers out of the woods and kick people off the beach. If you say too much about the fact that it's a public beach, you dramatically increase your chances of arrest. "I could arrest you for trespassing on public property, you know," says the enlightened police officer. That's a good one. How can a citizen of the public trespass on public property? But tell that to the cop and you'll be sleeping on a cold metal bench that night. Drive too fast or make a mistake on the road and you're pulled over, detained, and fined, and your insurance goes up for the next six years. Of course, any arrests, driving infractions, or subversive activity is noted on your permanent record. It is documented, stamped, numbered, filed, and added to the system's databases.

You've heard all the stories, so I won't bore you with them. The point is that government wants to keep you in line. If you fall out of line, you are made to believe it is because you have failed as a citizen. You are kept down. (What do some folks do who are kept down? They say, "Gee, I better go and join the army and get me some discipline or I ain't never gonna make nuthin' of myself.")

• ➤

You can easily see how these experiences shape and mold us into what society says we should be. What we really are and what we really feel about any of it is of little concern to the bureaucrats who administer the system.

Now that you have a more solid understanding of the word "identity" as it pertains to this book, we can move on to discuss the various reasons for changing it.

CHAPTER TWO

Your Identity—
Why Change It?

There are countless reasons why an individual may wish to establish a secondary identity. The reasons are as varied as the individuals who possess them. Some of these reasons may be "legitimate" in the eyes of society and some may not. It is not the purpose of this book to judge the individual's motives.

The reasons, though innumerable, do share one common tie—keeping ahead of the system. A growing number of people feel that government is too invasive, that we are looking down the throat of Big Brother, and our so-called privacy is quickly becoming a nostalgic notion. As you read through this book, you will begin to appreciate the constant tug-of-war that takes place as the system moves toward totalitarianism and a growing number of thinking people attempt to oppose, circumvent, and undermine this movement.

PURCHASING ALCOHOL

Perhaps one of the most popular reasons for obtaining counterfeit identity documents is for the purpose of procuring alcoholic beverages. Young adults are naturally curious about things, especially those that society says are "off limits." So, when a minor is slightly shy of the legal drinking age, the natural desire is to obtain ID that says otherwise and find out what alcohol is all about.

Young women can often get away with using their older sister's driver's license to get into nightclubs. Of course, young men can also borrow their older brother's ID to get into nightclubs, but it doesn't work as well for men.

There are a few reasons why women are more likely to experience success when "borrowing" an ID. For example, women are known, in fact expected, to change hairstyles and appearance often, sometimes on a daily basis. Therefore, when presenting her older sister's ID, a woman does not necessarily have to look exactly like the photograph on the ID.

Oftentimes, it is not even necessary for a woman to use the ID of a relative. Women that hang out in cliques often resemble each other to a great extent. If one woman is of legal drinking age, she can enter a nightclub and pass her ID back to an underage member of the group who resembles her. The underage woman can then reuse the same ID and get into the club. No? I've seen this done more than once.

When an underage male tries to present his older brother's ID at a bar or nightclub, he comes under much more scrutiny. A major reason for this has to do with the late maturity age of adolescent males. Many males between the ages of 17 and 19 still look like kids. When they attempt to use their older brother's ID, the photo may contain telltale signs that the bearer is not the person in the photograph. For instance, the older brother's photo may depict a postadolescent male bearing a five-o'clock shadow and clear complexion. The younger brother using this ID may lack significant facial hair and have an acne condition. This will cause the bouncer to send him on his way.

BANKING PRIVACY

Among the more sophisticated reasons for establishing an alternate identity is that of financial privacy. If you happen to have judgments against you such as alimony, child support, or creditor debt, it may be in your best interest to keep Aunt Hilda's generous bequest a secret from the rest of the world.

_ •

Just exactly what are you to do with that $10,000 check from the law firm of Dewey, Taycum & Howe? Well, you could deposit it into your savings account and wait for your ex-wife's attorney to do an asset check on you. Or you could use the techniques outlined in the following chapters to hide your windfall from those who would pry. The choice is yours.

Hiding a bequest is one thing; keeping money from your child is something else altogether. Only you know if you're paying enough money to support your child. This book is not intended to provide a means for noncustodial parents to avoid financial responsibility for their children. (Granted, many custodial parents view child support as their "livelihood" and, unfortunately, many courts support this notion.) If you use the techniques in this book, be fair. Whatever you do, don't disappear on your child. The bond you can form with your children is more valuable than any dollar amount society can take away from you.

RUNNING SCAMS

Planning on hitting up some nice credit card companies for some play money? Or maybe ordering up some utility services on the cuff for a year or two? Perhaps you are looking to sell some nonexistent aluminum siding while you are laid off next winter and living in a rent-free apartment. Whatever your game, it's probably not a good idea to go around flaunting your real name, address, and credentials—unless you're just in it for the short term and anxiously looking forward to some "time off" at the county's expense.

When the credit card company begins to wonder why you haven't made any payments toward your $7,500 in recent charges, it would be a lot better if they came pounding on the door of a mail drop, don't you think? When the cable police show up to snip your wire and grab their box, it would be nice if you could simply smile and say, "Oh, that bastard. Yes, my landlord had a bitch of a time getting him outta this place.

Matter of fact, I was supposed to move in a month ago and that SOB held me up. If you do find him, tell him that I'd like to have a word with him. Cable box? Don't see one here. Go ahead and snip away, though. The irony is, I was just going to call up and order some cable myself. Sure you want to snip that wire?"

CHECKOUT COUNTER CARDS

Many grocery stores are now offering "special discount cards" that automatically guarantee the user will receive credit for any coupons the store has published that week. The user no longer has to cut coupons out and present them to the cashier. A variation of this is that the cardholder's total purchase price is discounted a certain percentage if they "participate" in the card program.

Sounds like a bargain, right? After all, what do you have to lose?

I say that all you have to lose is your freedom, privacy, and eventually your sanity. What the grocery stores don't tell you is that the card is actually used to make a record of your buying habits, which is then exploited and sold to companies that compile mailing lists (see below).

Also, these cards will effectively determine just how much you are willing to pay for certain items. In this way, the merchant assures himself that he can squeeze every penny from you that he can.

These kinds of traps make it almost impossible to stay out of computer databases and off mailing lists. Hopefully, when you are done with this book, you will see just how information-hungry the world really is. You will then be able to live your life in such a way as to experience true personal freedom.

INFORMATION RESELLERS

Commercial information resellers make your personal information available to the general public. Items in these databases include last known address, mail forwarding address, magazine subscriptions, motor vehicle information, real property ownership, personal property ownership (such as boats, yachts, and airplanes), credit information, buying habits, average yearly income, number of children, marital status, court filings (including bankruptcy), judgments and civil filings, and much, much more.

MAIL PRIVACY

Want a quick way to sort your mail? Well, next time you're tempted by some piece of junk mail into ordering an "informative brochure," why not use an altered identity? By using a made-up name or, better yet, a misspelling of your real name and/or alteration of your address, you can easily identify all future junk mail that results from your responding to that one ad. Aside from the education that you'll receive regarding the marketing practices of Corporate America, you will gain the luxury of being able to sort your mail by subject simply by seeing how it's addressed.

For example, if you happen to reside at 180 Happy-Go-Lucky Lane and you become intrigued by the latest cure for baldness, respond to the ad using the return address 180B Happy-Go-Lucky Lane. Then, over the next 10 years when you are receiving junk mail from every bald scam in the world, you will throw it in the circular file as soon as you see the "B" in the address. This system works great for the individual with many interests. If you happen to be interested in art, boating, electronics. and music, you can reside at 180A, 180B, 180E, and 180M Happy-Go-Lucky Lane, respectively. The postman will still deliver the piece of mail to you as long as the altered name and address are close enough to the originals.

A similar system can be employed for advanced call screening. If the voice on the other end of the telephone happens to be inquiring as to the availability of a Mr. Jonathan Dough, we can ask, "Is that Jonathan Senior, Jonathan Junior, Jonathan the Third, or little John-John? What is this regarding?"

•━

"It's regarding that bridge in Brooklyn, sir."
"Oh, that'd be for Jonathan Junior. He just died."
"Okay, sorry to bother you." Click.

MAGAZINE SUBSCRIPTIONS

Mail privacy also spawns another nice advantage for the information-savvy identity changer. If you have mutated your name enough and have enough distinct personal and business identities at your residence, then you can continually receive "free trial" issues of your favorite magazines year round!

For example, if you happen to be interested in a magazine called *Identity Changing Times*, then you could take them up on their no-obligation free trial offer. Usually, you can squeeze about three issues out of these offers before the company insists on your payment in order to "continue receiving the benefit of" reading their magazine.

So, if you've established four distinct identities at your residence, have each identity, in turn, accept the magazine's free trial offer and then cancel it after three months. State on the bill, "CANCEL. Do not want. Did not order." They will always cancel the subscription and stop billing you because collection expenses would exceed what you owe them, and they would rather keep you on their subscription list to impress their advertisers. After all, a magazine does not really make any money by selling subscriptions per se. The real money is in convincing advertisers that a lot of people read their magazine and thus the advertiser should spend their advertising dollars with that magazine. So when one identity has exhausted the free trial period, spark up number two. When number two has worn out his welcome, have one of your business entities receive the magazine for awhile!

GENERAL PRIVACY

Changing your identity does not necessarily mean laser surgery, ties with the underworld, or taking four different taxis to work in the morning. Changing your identity could simply mean giving someone a fake name, address, and occupation. Certainly there are times when you are hesitant to give some store clerk your real phone number because their intentions are questionable. Or what about those lovely folks conducting polls or surveys? Do they really need to know who you are? Do you know who *they* really are?

How about dating? That can be risky business during the initial stages. Why offer complete strangers your real name and address? Remember the movie *Fatal Attraction*? If that's not a major incentive to keep your real identity private, then I don't know what is!

GOVERNMENT INVASION

The IRS (Internal Revenue Service, or "It's Really Slavery") now insists that all children listed as dependents or "qualifying children" on tax returns have a Social Security Number (SSN).

The Social Security Administration now indexes all "retired" Social Security Numbers in order to prevent unauthorized reuse of them. Quarterly circulars are made available to banks so that they may more easily recognize bogus SSNs.

Reciprocal agreements pertaining to the sharing of database information are being formed at an alarming rate between state, federal, and private bureaus. Child support enforcement divisions now share information with public welfare departments to track the whereabouts of noncustodial parents (NCPs), *whether or not* the NCP is in arrears.

PARANOID GOVERNMENT BUREAUS

Any individual or organized group not conforming to a strict social code is labeled as radical, subversive, and militant. FBI files are started, certain persons and groups are targeted for surveillance, and, if the feds get too nervous, we have another Waco on our hands.

19

PROFILING

Though we are supposed to live in a society where all men are created equal, where we are allegedly free to pursue life, liberty, and happiness, and where we are considered to be innocent until proven guilty, there are certain tactics used by government and law enforcement that make one wonder about the sincerity of all that.

For instance, the FBI, local police, and border patrols have established a system called "profiling." The system was initially developed by a psychiatrist as a means of catching bombers and serial killers. The concept is not a bad idea so long as its use is limited to catching existing felons who remain anonymous and at large.

The problem, not surprisingly, is that law enforcement has taken profiling to an abusive level. Hypothetical profiles of persons "likely" to commit a crime are now kept on file and, in fact, studied by law enforcement personnel.

If you're ever crossing the border between the United States and Canada, whether you're aware of it or not, your appearance is being judged and compared to profiles. There are so many people crossing the border that the border cops simply can't check all of them thoroughly. Ever wonder why some cars are searched more thoroughly than others? Profiles.

If you want an easy time crossing the border, you are best off driving a freshly washed late-model SAAB 900 with a clean interior, wearing a shirt and tie, and traveling with what appears to be a wife and two kids eagerly looking through site-seeing brochures. The border cops will say, "You're all set, have a nice trip."

However, if you're attempting to cross the border on a mud-spattered Harley Davidson, wearing you're bandanna and a Grateful Dead T-shirt from 12 years ago, with a long string of multicolored feathers roach-clipped to your handle bars, you can expect a closer inspection.

The above is a somewhat diametrical example of profiling

for the purpose of making a point. Some of you may say, "Yeah, no kidding. The dude on the Harley should be more suspect." Well, law enforcement takes this concept to extremes. According to their profiles, certain models of cars are more often driven by people who carry contraband and therefore more often searched. Certain ethnic groups are more likely to be drug smugglers. Certain hairstyles are associated with subversive activity. (Ever hear of skinheads?)

This is the essence of totalitarianism, my friends. The scary thing is that profiling is blindly accepted by most of society.

. . .

Now that we've enumerated some reasons for changing your identity, we can discuss some ways to accomplish this. We will begin by identifying the various ID documents. Then we will discuss how to acquire or manufacture them.

CHAPTER THREE

Identity Documents

We all know who we are. But how do we show others who we are? To a certain extent, others can see who we are. To most people, it is readily apparent if we are male or female. We are observably tall or short. Our racial origin is easily determined and, in some cases, our ethnic background is there for the world to see.

However, it is not readily apparent if someone is, say, a certified public accountant. Of course, I could tell you that I'm a CPA, and you may accept this. Chances are, though, if you were running a business and wanted to hire me to do your books, you would expect me to validate my claim that I am a CPA. In anticipation of this, most CPAs hang their certification in a frame on the wall of their office. This example demonstrates that, in society, identity documents show others facts about ourselves they may wish to know.

Sometimes, though, people "wish to know" more than we care to tell them. Brushing them off is usually, at least, uncomfortable and, at worst, the beginning of a heated argument. Fortunately, the identity changer has documents and tactics to help avoid such unpleasantries. In this chapter, we will explore how to obtain identity documents and how to use them to protect your privacy.

PART ONE: READILY AVAILABLE DOCUMENTS

An identity document is nothing more than a device used to demonstrate to another individual that you are who you say you are. As a society, we have a certain number of items that people typically use to accomplish this. The type of identity document necessary to perform the task will vary depending on whom you are trying to convince and of what you are trying to convince them.

Recently, I had accepted an offer from a certain manufacturer of postal metering machines. The offer allowed me to try their machine free for three months. If, after three months, I decided that I did not want to keep their machine, they would come pick it up and I would be under no further obligation.

So, I tried the machine out. After the free trial period, I decided that it would not be worth the rental expense. Accordingly, I called the company and, a week or two later, two service women showed up at my office to remove the machine.

Being a cautious individual, I asked one of the women if she had anything on her which would indicate that she was, if fact, a representative of the company in question. She showed me her clipboard, which contained a professionally printed invoice from her company that included my name, address, and account number. She then insisted on showing me her driver's license. I told her this was not necessary but nonetheless, she showed it. Shortly afterward, I carried the machine down to their truck, which had other machines from the same company in the back. I signed a few papers, got a receipt, and the transaction was concluded.

Reflecting upon this afterward, I thought it somewhat ironic that the girl insisted on showing me her driver's license. First of all, it was a testament to the fact that the driver's license has become the standard piece of "concrete" identification in the United States. The irony was that her driver's license in this particular instance was of little or no import. What I needed to know as a consumer was if I was releasing this expensive piece of machinery to the proper individual—the proper individual, in this case, being a representative of the company who owned the machine. As it turned out, the invoice and the other postal metering machines in the back of her truck were the "identification documents" that convinced me she was who she said she was. Her driver's license alone would not have accomplished this.

Of course, had she been a con artist, the "identifying documents" in question would have been fine examples of identity documents that are ridiculously easy to obtain, however specific to the cause they may have been.

I would like to begin our discussion of available identity documents by discussing other, more general, examples of such documents that are extremely easy to acquire.

DRIVER'S LICENSE:
DON'T BE A FOOL, GO TO SCHOOL!

In the United States, the driver's license has become the foremost means of positive identification. For the serious identity changer, a valid driver's license is an invaluable tool to have. Your new life will be so much easier once you possess one. However, obtaining a driver's license under an assumed identity is not as simple as walking into the Department of Motor Vehicles and getting your picture taken. The process involves obtaining a learner's permit, "learning" to drive for a period of at least six months, passing a written exam, and then taking a road test.

The advantage here is that so much emphasis is placed on verifying the road knowledge and driving skill of the applicant, there is much less emphasis on verifying his or her identity. The disadvantage is that there is a considerable amount of time involved and, in some states, the applicant must have a licensed driver accompany him or her during the road test. If you are planning to make a clean break, you probably don't want to enlist one of your friends to accompany you during your road test. Your friend will be wondering why you are taking the test when he has always known you as a licensed driver. He may also be curious as to why the examiner keeps calling you "Mr. Capone."

A parsimonious and elegant solution to this dilemma is to enroll in a driver's education program with a driving school. If you happen to be much older than your late teens or early twenties, it will look much less suspicious if you do this in an urban area. Due to the availability of public transportation, many folks who live in urban areas do not learn to drive until they are much older, if ever. To some, the entire process of enrolling in a driver's education program, attending classes, taking one-on-one driving instruction with a trainer, and then going for the "big day" to get a license may seem somewhat elaborate. But that's exactly the point. It's so elaborate that it shields your actual intention quite well. Besides, it's a lot easier to lie to a driving instructor than to a registry cop (most of the licensing preliminaries will be handled by the driving school).

CREDIT CARDS

Anybody who has a nicely manufactured work ID (see Chapter 6) and a Visa, Mastercard, or American Express is obviously a stand-up citizen and deserves a minimum of fuss when, for example, opening a checking account. (Details of opening a checking account will be presented in Chapter 7.)

But you can't get a credit card without proper credit, right? Wrong. When it comes to acquiring a clean credit card, there are two big loopholes that can be useful to the identity changer.

One convenient loophole is the secured credit card. Credit card companies, being greedy entities, will typically solicit secured accounts from individuals with poor credit or no credit at all. Of course, if you have good credit you can also get one, but why would anybody want to do that?

The safest way to do this is to establish a credit profile on the new "you" by using the techniques outlined in Chapter 8, then wait to be added to the mailing lists of secured credit card companies. An equally safe way is to call up such a company and ask them to send some literature and an application to your new address. WARNING: Do not do this from your old address, your old employer's address, or from anywhere connected with your past life (e.g., the address of a friend, relative, girlfriend, cell mate, etc.). Make sure that it is the "new you" making the call and giving the address and phone number of your new identity. Caller ID is a favorite database builder and fraud detector among banks and credit card companies.

(Credit card companies require you to call an 800 number to verify you received their credit card. The computer system answering the phone first tries to verify that the telephone number you are calling from is the same number you gave as your home phone number on your credit application. If it is, you are then required to punch in your Social Security Number and perhaps some other verifying information about yourself, such as your mother's maiden name. If the number you are calling from cannot be verified as your home number, the computer system generally gives you the message, "Your call is being transferred to an account representative," or something of that nature. The representative will ask questions of a more scrutinizing nature regarding your identity, as flag for potential fraud has been raised. Be forewarned!)

Another way of obtaining a credit card as ID is to add a cardholder to your existing account. Of course, this account must be in good standing and stay in good standing throughout the process of spawning a new credit profile. American Express is the best company for doing this because they maintain their own credit database and are exceptionally hungry for information. AMEX insists on having the new cardholder's Social Security Number so that they can start up a profile on that person. (Acquiring a new Social Security Number will be discussed later in this chapter.)

This will get you three things for the person you wish to create: a piece of identification; a credit profile established with AMEX, which is eventually sent out to credit information services such as TRW, EQUIFAX, and TRANSUNION; and, most importantly, a good credit history transferred to the new you.

Why is this important? Well, the new credit profile will state that "another party is liable for this account." However, if all payments are made on time, the owner of the new credit profile will eventually start receiving preapproved credit card offers. The time frame for this is usually 6 to 18 months. When this happens, accept the preapproved offers and immediately stop using the first credit card altogether. Also, the "old you" should cancel the credit card originally used to spawn this credit profile after it's been completely paid off. Since credit reporting agencies are primarily interested in maintaining a database of negative credit, the old account will eventually be removed from your credit profile.

This is all beautiful, right? Well, that depends on just why it is you want to create this new person (see Chapter 1). If your intent is to get lost forever, *do not use this approach*. While it is certainly feasible that the connection between your "real" credit profile and the new credit profile may eventually be buried so deep as to render it economically unfeasible for anybody to bother to trace, *it is not a clean break!* When you use the new credit card to open a checking account under your new identity, the clerk may make a photocopy of your ID as well as a memo of the account number imprinted on the credit card. This loose thread back to the old you is not the kind of thing you want to have floating about in cyberspace.

Again, if the new you stays clean, you may never have a problem. But consider your sanity. When you make a break, you want to make a clean break. Otherwise, you will always be wondering if someone has used your loose ends to track you down. What if, for example, somebody hired me to find you? With that credit card connection, I would be able to find you quickly. You will always have that insecurity in the back of your head. Isn't this what you were attempting to get away from to begin with? I hope you heed my warnings.

～•

SOCIAL SECURITY CARD

Once you decide on which SSN to use for your new identity (see Part Three of this chapter), you can then deal with the relatively simple process of producing the Social Security card. The insignia on your typical Social Security card consists of an American bald eagle holding a box in which your Social Security Number is printed. There are lots of companies around that will print your SSN, or any SSN, on such a card for a nominal charge. Or, you could always photocopy someone else's card, then white-out their SSN and type in your own. Then, photocopy the amended card and laminate it. Color copies work best with this approach.

Here is a favorite trick of mine. Ever see those life insurance companies that offer you a nice Social Security card with your number on it simply for requesting their information packet? The offer does not even need to be addressed to you! Simply fill out the information request form with the desired name, address, and SSN. The company will be happy to add you to their database, and you will receive a nice, credit-card-sized piece of plastic complete with the eagle insignia, your name, and your SSN. This adds a nice touch to your portfolio of identity documents. Also, this will place you on a few junk mailing lists, which is a nice additional benefit if you have a mail drop and you want your flow of mail to appear ordinary there.

PHONE, ELECTRIC, AND GAS BILLS

Though not normally thought of as identity documents, there are a few times when these little buggers can come in handy. When relocating under a new identity, you will undoubtedly have your utilities turned on in your new name at your new address. Chapter 4 enumerates the different options an identity changer should consider before establishing a new residence. Your need, or lack of need, for utility bills will of course factor into your decision. Obviously, you can't turn the electricity on in a mail drop. Also, answering services do not bill you in the traditional way in which the telephone company bills you.

As you will learn in Chapter 8, having a phone in your own name often gives you an edge when applying for credit. Moreover, you will find that it is very difficult to order a copy of your credit report without proof of address. Usually, the credit reporting agency will readily accept a utility bill as proof of address.

Another instance where a utility bill comes in handy is when opening bank accounts. One bank I deal with will not open a bank account for you unless you present two forms of identification. One, they say, must be a driver's license and the other a utility bill. I went so far as to ask the accounts manager if a credit card or birth certificate would do. The answer on both counts was "no." Granted, you could make a big stink about how you don't drive, never did as a matter of fact, and while we're on the subject, I don't believe in electricity; oh, and by the way, I'm part Amish, and isn't there some law against this? Eventually, they will grease you so you don't squeak, to borrow from the old adage. But do you really want to generate that kind of attention when opening a bank account under an assumed identity? If you get a hard time, simply go elsewhere. Or, if you happen to have the necessary documents . . .

Also, utility bills, when strategically deployed as innocent trash on the backseat of your car or on the front and back dashboards, make for much less question answering during routine traffic stops, if you catch my drift.

Of course it never hurts if you just happen to be carrying a bunch of bills that need paying when, let's say, you're stopping by the local Social Security office, county clerk's office, or vital statistics registry. Placing them innocently on the counter at a convenient angle while speaking with the clerk will provide an excellent subliminal base from which you can manipulate your friendly bureaucrat. Of course, "manipulate" is meant in the most loving, humanitarian sense of the word.

BAPTISMAL CERTIFICATE: DON'T EMBARRASS ME!

Several books on the subject of identity changing seem to hail the baptismal certificate as some type of boon to those of us interested in changing our identity. This notion had some merit many years ago when the system was experiencing true prosperity and fewer of us had to resort to tricking it to make a buck. These days, the baptismal certificate simply doesn't fly. The Social Security Administration won't even accept a baptismal certificate as secondary ID. Its application states that it will accept a "church membership or confirmation record (if not used as evidence of age)." That's as close as they get to accepting a baptismal certificate.

Despite my skepticism, I thought that I'd lend this baptismal certificate enough credence to actually conduct some field research on the matter. To make the experiment as sound as possible, I used my actual baptismal certificate as opposed to a forgery or reprint. My mother pulled it out from my "Baby Days" book, where it had been stuffed decades ago and hadn't been seen since. I attempted to use this form of identity in the following situations:

- Purchasing alcohol
- Entering a club
- Cashing a check
- Using a credit card

Now tell me, how many strange looks did I get that day? Have *you* ever carried around your baptismal record as proof of identity? Think about it.

LIBRARY CARDS AND FINISHING TOUCHES

Sometimes referred to as "ancillary documentation," lesser forms of identification should not be taken lightly. Aside from a driver's license, credit card, and Social Security card, most people have other forms of ID in their wallets. Since most folks don't consider these other documents as being identification, it is very easy for the novice identity changer to ignore having them in his possession. However, if all you have is a brand new driver's license, credit card, and Social Security card in your wallet, most bureaucrats would find this highly suspicious. So scuff up that license, send that Social Security card through the wash a couple of times, and get some use out of that credit card. Then, begin collecting some of these "lesser" forms of identification:

Wallet Insert

This one's a gimme—it comes with the wallet. What more could you possibly ask for? Fill it out with any specifics you desire. For example:

Doctor Larry C. Fine
123 Stooge Terrace
New Rochelle, NY 10017
"Reward if found and returned intact"

For an extra special touch, add the monogram LCF to the wallet!

Library Card

You really should have one anyway. It's probably not a good idea to use your old one while living under a new identity. In fact, it's probably a good idea to have a few library cards under different identities, depending on what you're into.

Ever see the movie *Seven*? There was a scene where the cops were out of leads and the bad guy was about to get away. (Sounds like a lot of movies, doesn't it?) So, the senior cop on the case examines the perpetrator's modus operandi. It turns out that the perp is seeking out the most egregious violators of the seven deadly sins, torturing them for extended periods of time, and finally executing them. The senior detective can see by the perp's MO that he possesses a great deal of knowledge pertaining to certain cult activities and decides the guy must be frequenting the library for reference material. He then informs the junior detective about a secret FBI database. According to the senior detective, the FBI targets certain literature in the library and tracks the name and address of any patron checking out the material. Apparently, how-to books on such topics as building a car bomb, screwing the government, the ins and outs of counterfeiting U.S. currency, identity changing, and the like are not favorites of the FBI.

Just a movie, you say? Well movies often contain information of this nature, and to date, I have yet to see a movement by the federal government to refute these implied allegations. I guess silence is best.

Jewelry, Jackets, and *Laverne and Shirley*

A few ornamental things can help to wrap up a new identity. By using engraved jewelry, class rings, monogrammed articles of clothing, and accessories, the identity changer can complete the image of being who he says he is. If you are going to be Buffalo Bill for a few years, it's a nice touch to get a windbreaker with "Buffalo Construction Company" embroidered on the back of it. This is much better than simply wearing a name tag that says "Buffalo Bill." Also, if you happen to be calling yourself Billy the Kid these days, it doesn't make a whole lot of sense to be wearing a jacket that explicitly states you are, in fact, Jack the Ripper.

In the real world, people do things. They have businesses and hobbies, play sports, or are otherwise enthused by cars, motorcycles, roller coasters, or pig farming. Most people work their identity into what they do. They don't even think about it. So, instead of just saying that you are indeed Mack the Knife, you will make a better impression by wearing a 1920s black sharkskin suit and keeping your teeth real white.

Let's not overdo it, though. If you walk into a bank and you have the Elvis tattoo, necktie, necklace, bracelet, jacket, monogrammed wallet, guitar sack, and secret decoder ring, the effect may turn out to be the opposite of what you intended.

I once heard it said that we all know what the "L" stands for on Laverne DiFazzio's sweater in the 1970s sitcom *Laverne and Shirley*. This is a fine example of mixing subtlety with high visibility.

PART TWO: BIRTH CERTIFICATES

Before delving into the logistics of whose birth certificate you should be obtaining, we should first discuss how easy it is to get a certified copy of *any* birth certificate your identity-changing heart desires. Every U.S. state or commonwealth, including Washington, D.C., has at least one registry of vital statistics. The vital statistics office is the central clearinghouse for all birth, marriage, and death records on file in every county in that state. The atmosphere at your average vital statistics office is pleasantly bureaucratic, and I strongly suggest patronizing it when you finally decide who the hell it is you want to be.

Why go to the big, scary, bureaucratic state agency instead of to the town or county clerk? Well, two reasons immediately come to mind. One, at the state level there is much less of a chance that the bureaucrat will have personally known our deceased subject. Certainly, we would not want to walk into the town clerk's office professing to be Iggy Piggy and demanding his birth certificate, only to glance down at the clerk's nameplate and see "Iggy Piggy, Senior—Town Clerk" forbiddingly engraved in low-grade aluminum.

The second reason is that you will have a strong psychological advantage when dealing with the predictable state bureaucrat. Since you know certain things about his behavior—specifically, his desire to both exercise power over you and brownnose his superiors by selling you something you don't need and thus making a quick $6 for the state—he can be manipulated easily.

I will show you how this works by first demonstrating how it doesn't work. If you definitely want to get a hard time, try this approach. Go into your state's vital statistics office and say, "Hello, I would like a certified copy of Iggy Piggy's birth certificate, please." A typical response from the bureaucrat would be, "Why? Who the hell are you? Are you Iggy Piggy? Why do you want a certified copy of his birth certificate?" Of course, the birth certificate is a public document, but try telling this to the bureaucrat.

Now try it using what you know about the psychological makeup of the typical bureaucrat. Walk up to him meekly and act stupid so he will know how superior he is. Say, "Um, I was just doing some genealogical research and I found a birth record that I would like a plain photocopy of." He will respond in a superior tone to show you how little you know, "We can't issue photocopies. We only issue certified copies at a charge of $6 per copy." You then respond, "Golly, well I'm new at this. There's really no other way?" He will educate you by telling you that of course there is no other way. We just can't go issuing photocopies of birth certificates with all the fraud that goes on these days, you know. With that you simply respond, "Oh, well I guess if there's no other way, I'll have to pay the fee. Hopefully my client will understand and reimburse me." You will have a certified copy of "your" birth certificate in a few minutes at a fee of roughly $6 in most states.

PART THREE: THE SOCIAL SECURITY NUMBER

Several books on the subject of identity changing hail the birth certificate as the "cornerstone" or "benchmark" of a person's identity. In my entire adult life, I have yet to have a bureaucrat request my birth certificate as a form of identification. Granted, for certain key documents such as a driver's license or passport, a birth certificate is needed during the application process. But for day-to-day living, it is the Social Security Number that is most often requested by banks, credit card companies, police departments, municipal offices, motels, automobile rental agencies, and just about anybody who wants to keep tabs on you.

Like everything else bureaucrats desire to keep track of, human beings have been serialized. Once established, your Social Security Number is the serial number that stays with you for the rest of your life.

A BRIEF HISTORY

United States Code Title 42, Section 301 *et sequentia* (and those that follow) brought the Social Security Act into existence in 1935. The program was allegedly established as a kind of forced retirement plan to provide for the general welfare of individuals who reach the age of retirement or become disabled and can no longer provide for themselves.

Under the plan, all individuals deriving income from salary, wages, tips, commissions, or self-employment must pay a portion of their earnings into a Social Security account. Each wage earner has a unique account with the Social Security Administration (SSA), which is identified by his Social Security Number (SSN).

The SSN is used to keep track of an individual's earnings on a quarterly basis. Upon a person's disability or retirement, the records are used to determine the dollar amount of monthly benefits that will be paid to the individual. In short, the more you pay into Social Security, the more you will get when you become eligible to collect benefits.

Regulations were also promulgated relative to the issuance of Social Security cards and the order in which SSNs should be assigned. It is these regulations that are of particular concern to identity changers.

WHY IS THIS IMPORTANT?

Typically, books on the subject of identity changing fail to establish the importance of the SSN as an identifier and its impact on the privacy of the individual. In fact, some books actually insist that the SSN is not an identifier. Though it may be true that the SSN was not *designed* as a general identifier (I have my doubts), it is certainly erroneous to state that it has not become one. I've read suggestions to "make up" a SSN and that the SSN is "no big deal." Prior to the 1980s, there may have been some truth to these claims. However, with government's increasing desire to reduce acts of fraud, the identity changer will certainly want to keep the following laws in mind:

A 1981 amendment to Section 208(g) of the Social Security Act makes it a criminal offense to:

- Alter, buy, sell, or counterfeit a Social Security card.
- Possess a genuine or counterfeit Social Security card with intent to sell or alter it.

Additionally, violations of Section 208 were changed from misdemeanors to felonies by the following provision:

- All violations of Section 208 of the Social Security Act committed after December 29, 1981, are felonies with penalties of up to $5,000 fine, up to 5 years in jail, or both.

In 1982, the False Identification Crime Control Act added Section 1028 to Title 18 of the United States Code, which provides for penalties of "not more than $25,000 or imprisonment for not more than 5 years, or both" for particular offenses involving false identification documents. The section clearly defines an identification document as "any document commonly accepted for the purpose of identification of individuals." Therefore, Social Security cards would be included under this Section. See Appendix C for the entire text of Section 1028.

Even as early as 1976, the Tax Reform Act amended Section 208(g) of the Social Security Act, making it a federal criminal offense to misuse a SSN for any reason. Prior to that, only issues of fraud against the SSA were addressed.

In addition to the above laws and potential penalties for misuse of the SSN, there are other significant reasons why the identity changer will want to take care in choosing a number.

Using the Social Security Death Index (SSDI), credit report-ing agencies cross-reference SSNs of deceased individuals with their existing credit profiles. If the SSN you invent happens to belong to a deceased person, there is a good chance your cred-it report will be flagged for potential fraud. Believe me, you don't need this kind of flag in your new life.

Care must also be taken when establishing a bank account with an acquired SSN. Banks may receive bulletins from the Social Security Administration that indicate the most recently issued SSNs. A 50-year-old man who walks into a bank with a SSN issued last quarter, or not yet issued, would be suspect.

Also, the IRS sends out a watch list of fraudulent SSNs to banks and other entities. The banks are supposed to search for accounts and safe deposit boxes connected with the SSNs on this circular.

After reading the above laws, regulations, and policies, it should be obvious that great care is needed in inventing, choos-ing, and using a Social Security Number.

CONSTRUCTION OF THE SSN

Some books on the subject of identity changing do explain the significance of the first three digits of the SSN. Unfortun-ately, the explanation stops there and is very limited even at that. Here is a detailed explanation of the entire SSN.

The SSN is a nine-digit number separated by two dashes into three segments. The first segment is comprised of three dig-its and, with the exception of the 700 series, indicates the area of the country in which the number was issued. (The 700 series was reserved for railroad retirement use.) This segment is referred to as the "area" segment. The middle segment is com-prised of two digits and is used to break the numbers from each area into groups. This segment is known as the "group" or "block" segment. The last segment is comprised of four digits and is used to serialize ten thousand numbers (0001 through 9999) within each group. This is called the "serial" or "serial number" segment. Thus we have:

〜•

AREA—BLOCK—SERIAL NUMBER
arranged as:
aaa-bb-ssss
where a = area, b = block, and s = serial number

When dealing with bureaucrats, it is important for the identity changer to understand the significance of each segment of the Social Security Number.

The area segment of the SSN indicates to the bureaucrat where the number was issued. If an uninformed identity changer invents a SSN beginning with 035, a savvy bureaucrat may know that this number should have been issued in the state of Rhode Island. The particularly cunning bureaucrat may make light conversation with the identity changer, inquiring as to where he grew up and places he may have lived. If the uninformed identity changer gets caught up in this phony conversation and unwittingly admits that he's never been in Rhode Island, the bureaucrat will become very suspicious. By the same token, if the identity changer invents a SSN that should have been issued in Alabama, yet he speaks with a strong Long Island accent, this may also raise suspicions in the savvy bureaucrat. When inventing a Social Security Number, you will want to use the area listings found in Appendix A while keeping the above caveats in mind.

With a little planning, it is a relatively simple task to obtain or invent a SSN that contains the proper first three digits needed for your intended purposes (i.e., where your new identity claims to be from). Choosing or finding a SSN with the appropriate block segment is somewhat more involved.

In many of the books I've read on this subject, the middle two digits of the SSN are purported to have little import. This is simply not the case. These digits give bureaucrats an idea of when the number was issued. In fact, look at a copy of your credit report sometime. You will find a line that states, "The Social Security Number you gave us was issued between 1956 and 1958" (the actual years may vary). What would be the point of inventing a credit profile that has your birth year as 1964 and your SSN as being issued in 1952? Such a contradiction would flag your report for potential fraud.

That line of your credit report is generated by computer software that compares the middle two digits of your SSN with an in-house database. This type of software and databasing is becoming more and more common. Variations of this software have been implemented as "Project Clean Data" by many state and federal agencies and is used to identify incorrect, unissued, and fraudulently used SSNs.

I have yet to come across a complete, up-to-date listing that details the year of issue for each block segment by state (or area). I have been compiling my own list over the years, albeit somewhat incomplete.

I have learned, and verified through experience, that within each area, odd groupings from 01 through 09 were the first issued and thus were probably issued before 1940. After the 09 block has been used, even numbers from 10 through 98 are issued. Then, as more numbers are needed, even groupings from 02 through 08, then odd groupings from 11 through 99 are issued.

The main thing that the identity changer needs to be concerned with is this: in which year was a particular block of numbers issued in your target area? The book *Social Security Number Fraud* published by Eden Press has a 25-page listing that you may wish to use as a reference. As long as the block, or middle two digits, of "your" SSN was issued after the year in which you claim to have been born, you have solid ground to stand on when presenting the SSN to bureaucrats.

Eden's listing is too long to reproduce here, and it is only valid from 1951–1978. Some of you may want to purchase Eden's book or may want more customized information. Knowing this, I have included some guidelines for compiling a SSN database of your own.

Making Your Own Database
The best way to gain a solid understanding of how your

state assigns SSNs is to create your own database. To accomplish this, take a notebook and pen with you to the vital statistics office in your state and begin looking through a book of death certificates. To find a recent book, get hold of the most recent index and write down some book numbers from it. Then, find the appropriate book or books.

You will notice that the death certificates indicate the decedent's SSN and age at time of death. These are the two bits of information in which you are primarily interested. Enter the SSN in one column of your notebook and the age of the decedent in an adjacent column. Be sure to enter the age the person would be if he or she were still alive, not the age at time of death. This is the reason for using a recent book of death certificates. With a recent book, you will have no need to compensate for the time that has elapsed since the death record was recorded. However, many states have a backlog, and the most recent book may not yet be available. If this is the case, grab a book that is exactly one year old and be sure to add one year to all of the given ages on the death certificates.

After you compile a sufficient amount of information, take your notebook home and enter the two columns into a database on your computer. Enter the SSNs in one field and the decedents' ages in an adjacent field just as you did in your notebook. It would be interesting to break the SSN into its three component parts and insert these into three separate fields. Then, you can sort the fields by the first three digits, middle two digits, or last four digits to see what kinds of patterns emerge. You are mainly interested in seeing which ages are associated with which middle two digits. The actual year of issue is not all that important for our purposes. We only need a general idea of what SSNs will be valid for the identity we are planning to create.

By the way, if you happen to own a laptop PC, you could create your database right at the vital statistics office and save yourself a step. This is public information, and as long as you don't scan documents into your PC, the bureaucrats should not have a problem with your using a laptop in the research room.

• ⤳

	AREA	BLOCK	AGE	DOD
1	019	52	26	1/1/97
2	014	38	40	1/1/97
3	019	22	65	1/1/97
4	101	26	56	1/1/97
5	110	26	60	1/1/97
6	119	60	20	1/1/97
7	210	56	22	1/1/97
8	224	90	35	1/1/97
9	282	40	83	1/1/97

This method should prove useful to anybody who is willing to take the time to compile the information. My database is compiled from actual credit reports I have reviewed and from credit profiles I have created or helped others to create. Obviously, this is the most accurate method. I realize, though, that not everybody is a private detective, and that is why I have included the substitute method above.

Another method of determining a SSN's year of issue is to just go ahead and use it in a request for a credit report. When you receive the report, it will tell you the year that the SSN was issued. Then, if the birth date that you used doesn't jibe with the number, simply send in the "Dispute Form" with an amended birth date. The credit bureau will be more than pleased that you have helped them make their files more accurate! Even if it turns out that the SSN is not useful for your specific needs, you will learn something about how the numbers were issued in your state. In this way, you can begin to compile your own database.

Highest Numbers Issued

Another thing with which the identity changer has to be concerned is the fact that banks and other bureaucratic agencies receive quarterly bulletins that show the highest issued SSNs by area. Thus, the middle two digits you choose must not be too high for the area you choose. Appendix B has a listing that was accurate as of January 1, 1993, which should be sufficient for most purposes.

However, if it is not, the techniques outlined in the "Making Your Own Database" section above can also be used to determine the highest SSNs issued in your area. Simply make a database of young people (with SSNs) who have died recently. This will give you a good idea as to the highest block issued in your area.

Summarizing the Construction of a SSN

Use the above information to make sure that the SSN you invent, borrow, or obtain has the following:

- Valid area number that supports the claims of your new identity.
- Valid block number that was *not* issued prior to the date on which you claim to have been born.
- Valid block number that is *not higher* than the highest number issued for the "area" segment of the SSN you are borrowing or inventing.
- Valid serial number (*not* 0000).

APPLYING FOR A SSN

The other option for obtaining a SSN is to actually apply for one under your new identity. This method offers several advantages if you are intending to disappear for good. If you use this method, you will have fewer hassles gaining and maintaining employment under your new identity. Also, when you retire, you can collect Social Security benefits, providing the program is still in existence.

The problem with this method is that most identity changers are too old to be applying for a SSN. Though one is never legally too old to apply for a SSN, most folks have obtained one by the time they are 15 years old. So, a 30-year-old man applying for a new SSN would appear conspicuous.

Of course you know that I wouldn't leave you without a nice little loophole out of this quandary. So here it is . . .

If the person applying for a SSN is under 18 years of age, application may be made via U.S. mail. The Social Security

Administration requires that you submit original documents or certified copies of the following:

- Your birth certificate
- Some form of identity, such as a driver's license, school record, medical record, or any of the following: U.S. government or state employee ID card; passport; school ID card, record, or report card

Using the methods outlined above in the section on birth certificates, you will want to adopt the BC of a person who:

- Died very young
- Did not have a SSN
- Would be 16–17 years old today

Now you have a valid birth certificate meeting the first requirement of the SSA. The next logical step is to create a secondary ID that is acceptable to the SSA. The safest choice is a school ID card. They are easy to create and are not standardized. Use the methods in Chapter 6 to create a school ID card that contains the following information:

- *Name of school.* Be sure to use a real school that is located in the town where you claim to reside (i.e., where your mail drop is).
- *"Your" name.*
- *Student ID number.*
- *YOG.* This is the year of graduation, which all bureaucrats abbreviate YOG. Use a YOG that is the same year in which you are applying for the SSN. This will make it look consistent with the ruse that we will use below.
- *Photo.* Be sure to use the photograph of a high school student here. If you happen to have someone's old high school ID (not your own), you can use the photo from that. If not, you will need to find another source such as a high school

yearbook. Or hire a teenager for some job and tell him he must bring two passport photos for his work ID. Use one for his work ID and the other one for "your" high school ID.

A nice touch on a high school ID is to add some trivial information to the back of it such as homeroom number, bus shift, school address and hours, etc. Of course, if you have some other form of secondary ID to offer the SSA, by all means use it!

What to Send the SSA

You are now going to write to the SSA and submit your identity documents. Use a piece of yellow lined paper and a cheap blue pen to write your note. If the pen happens to be a little leaky, that helps too. You are trying to create the image that you are, indeed, a high school student.

In your note to the SSA, state that you are in need of a SSN because your parents told you to get a job, or you need a job so that you can buy a car, go to the prom, pay for college, or whatever. Just make it sound like a teen is writing the letter. Tell the SSA that you have "sent them the documents that they told you to send" or similar wording as would be used by a teenager. *Do not* begin the letter, "Enclosed please find the documents necessary to facilitate issuing . . ." This would give you away as an experienced letter writer, which most high school students are not.

What I'm about to tell you to do may seem strange. In fact, it may seem like suicide. In your letter to the SSA, include the address of the school "in case you have any questions." It may also help to include the phone number and the name of a guidance counselor at the school.

What? What if they call? I hear your panic. The idea is to make the application look as legitimate as possible. A teenager is not used to dealing with bureaucracies and would want the SSA to call the school if there are any problems. But of course, you know there are no problems with the application. The only potential problem is that the SSA bureaucrat may be suspicious of fraud, right? Well, when you include the school address and phone number, the lazy bureaucrat will think, "Hey, who would give me the school address and phone number if they were trying to commit fraud?" Hopefully, the bureaucrat will OK your application and go to lunch.

When you are done composing your letter, send it to the SSA field office in your state capital. Do not use a field office local to the school you are claiming to attend, as the bureaucrats there may be familiar with the school and/or its IDs. Also, don't just send your application to a field office on the other side of the state. It would look suspicious if you sent your application to anywhere but your local field office or the state capital. The office at the capital expects to get mail from all over the state, whereas local field offices expect only local mail.

The best time to apply is late spring to early summer when the SSA is busy filling many requests similar to yours. One caveat for the not-so-brazen: be aware of the possibility that a savvy SSA bureaucrat may have already processed SSN applications from the same school. If that applicant also used his or her school ID to apply, the bureaucrat may wonder why your ID looks different. If possible, get a peek at a legitimate ID prior to creating yours.

Covering Your Bases

The above scenario should work most of the time. Yes, that's most of the time. The other side of the coin is that the bureaucrat may call the school to see if there really is a Jonathan Derringer, student ID# 01234, who attends their school and takes bus number five home to Clarkesville. If this happens, your application will be denied and an investigation may or may not be conducted.

If you suspect that this has happened, abandon your mail drop and start the process over again. The best approach is to establish a few mail drops all at the same time and use each one to apply for a SSN, using separate identities for each. This is like a direct marketing approach and will yield you at least one SSN.

Under no circumstances should you use the same mail drop for more than ten SSNs. Under the SSA's "Project Map," if more than ten Social Security cards are mailed to the same address, a computer at the SSA will flag that address for potential fraud. I strongly recommend using one address for each application.

MOVING ON

Before we move on to the finer points of establishing residence, gaining education, and setting up business entities, I'd like to leave you with the following.

The above information pertaining to birth certificates and Social Security Numbers varies greatly by state and is constantly changing. Always bear in mind that there is a constant need for updated solutions to the identity problem. Be sure to stay on top of your research.

~·

CHAPTER FOUR

Establishing Residence

~·

A new identity wouldn't be foolproof if you stayed in the same place. Even if you're not skipping town, your new identity needs to be associated with a new residence. In modern society, a residence is really comprised of two things: a street address and a telephone number.

PART ONE: ADDRESS

A street address, whether or not associated with an actual building, renders the impression that you have a home or, more important to the bureaucrat, a "situs"—a place where you can be found, contacted, taxed, policed, harassed, and generally accessible to Big Brother. Sounds like fun, right? So let us explore how to keep our information-hungry friends happy . . .

MAIL DROPS

A mail drop is an establishment that rents mailbox space much like the U.S. Post Office rents post office boxes. There are two advantages typical to mail drop establishments. One advantage is that the mail drop facility allows its "tenants" to use its full street address, such as 1313 Mockingbird Lane, and then add the mailbox number as a "suite" number. This yields an address that looks like:

Mr. Frank N. Stein
1313 Mockingbird Lane, Suite 39
Transylvania, PA 12345

The middle line of this address looks much more "established" than if it read P.O. Box 1313. The U.S. Postal Service does not allow its box holders this advantage.

Because of this established look, many entrepreneurs employ the services of mail drops for purposes of appearing, well, established. If you were to use a mail drop for this purpose, it would be best to find one located on a main road. A business with an address of 1100 Main Street, Suite 201, sounds professional and established. Conversely, if you want your mail drop to give the impression of an actual residence, a less businesslike address would be in order. To create the illusion of a residence, avoid business-sounding roads such as Main Street, Kings Highway, or Avenue of the Americas. Also, you may choose to use "Apartment 2" or "Unit 12" as opposed to a suite number if your goal is to appear more residential.

Often, picking up the mail on a daily basis becomes inconvenient for the "tenant." This brings us to the second advantage of using a mail drop establishment: mail forwarding. Many mail drops, for an additional service charge, will package up your mail on a weekly basis and forward it to you at your "real" address. This address could be another mail drop if you happen to be involved in some heavy scheme or are simply of the more paranoid genre. You decide how much anonymity you want. It may suit your needs best to pick up your own mail and eliminate any paper trail. Some mail drops have 24-hour access, and these are recommended if you'd rather not be on a first-name basis with the hired help. Got it?

Since it is becoming more common for people to use mail drops to trick government agencies, insurance companies, and creditors, it is also becoming more common for bureaucrats to maintain databases of known mail drops. If you apply for Social Security or a tax refund through a known mail drop, you may be receiving your application back unprocessed.

Knowing that databasing mail drops is becoming common among bureaucrats, it would be nice if there were a way to have the luxury of a mail drop without the risk of the world finding out about it. Fortunately, there is.

The condominium where I live has outside mailboxes for each unit. You've seen them—they are the big aluminum cubes that contain 16 mailboxes each. My building happens to have 30 units, which requires two cubes, or 32 mail boxes. Gee, there just happens to be two leftover boxes. One is used for outgoing mail. Would you like to take a guess as to who uses the other one?

Granted, it would probably be a bad idea to invent an entire condominium unit on the route of a veteran mail carrier. If the mail carrier has had the route for any length of time, he may become suspicious of the new unit box. But, if you know of a mail carrier who happens to be retiring soon, you may want to check out his route to see which condominiums he delivers to. Overwhelmed and anxious to learn the route, the new delivery person won't blink twice when delivering mail to unit number 31!

Know of any vacant lots or abandoned buildings? While the post office won't deliver to these addresses, you can still use them for some purposes. Use the address as your residence but file a mail forwarding card with the post office. Have the mail delivered wherever you like, depending on your needs. Anybody can file a mail forwarding card—you do not have to prove prior residence, nor do you have to file the card in person. It can all be done—you guessed it—through the mail!

ESTABLISHING ACTUAL RESIDENCE

If you've decided that you're opting out of this mess and starting a new life under a new identity, you will want to establish an actual residence as opposed to just a mail drop. The identity documents you obtain will determine if you can buy a home under your new identity. For instance, if you do not yet have a valid driver's license under your new identity, you are probably not ready to purchase a home through the usual channels of real estate acquisition.

When buying a home through the usual channels, there are lawyers and real estate agents involved. These people may ask you for identity-verifying documents or information at various stages of the transaction. However, the only point of a real estate transaction where there will be a legitimate need for actual identity documents will be at the closing. The attorneys will want to have notarized signatures from both the buyer and seller. Practically speaking, it is more important that the signature of the seller be notarized than the signature of the buyer. The buyer's attorney wants to be sure that the person collecting thousands of dollars from his client is indeed the true owner of the property. Attorneys are nothing more than low-level bureaucrats. So, you can expect that the attorney for the seller will, by nature, expect a notarized signature from the buyer as well. The usual identity document requested for notarization is a driver's license.

Remember, the above rules hold true if you intend to go through the usual channels for buying property. But there are several ways to buy property. Though they are typically associated with real estate transactions, neither an attorney nor a real estate agent is necessary to complete one. In fact, many states don't even require a notarized signature on the deed, nor is title to a property necessarily invalid if it is not filed with the county. In these states, such formalities are still considered preventative measures. The courts do not want ordinary people to lose their property for failure to comply with certain technicalities. Check your state's applicable laws.

A NICE ALTERNATIVE

In the United States, the real estate market peaked around

1987. Throughout the 1980s, condominium prices were pushed up into the price range of small houses. It was not uncommon for people to pay $80,000 to $120,000 to purchase a condominium. When the economy began to recess, people started moving back toward the cities, and many young people moved back home with their parents. Condominium associations over the next few years lost owners through foreclosures at an alarming rate. At that time, these associations were not entitled to collect back condo fees unless there was money left over from the foreclosure sale. In nearly all foreclosures, though, the money taken in from the sale was not even enough to satisfy the outstanding mortgage. The primary mortgage holder was entitled to all of the proceeds from the foreclosure sale in order to satisfy the note they were holding. Thus, any back fees owed to the association went unpaid.

Without sufficient income from condo fees, the associations were unable to pay for the common area expenses such as building and property maintenance, repairs, water and sewer bills, and property taxes. In severe cases, associations were unable to hire a management company to tend to the daily affairs of the association.

The condo associations were further jeopardized as the owners, now laid-off from work, abandoned their units altogether. With fewer and fewer owners paying in, the associations were forced to raise their fees in order to keep up with taxes, building maintenance, and management services. This caused more owners to leave as they could no longer afford the high condo fees on top of the inflated mortgage they were holding.

Many associations collapsed, forming ghost towns or slum areas. The condominium market itself collapsed, and people, out of utter fear, stopped investing in them.

Some states saw this problem and decided to pass laws that would help turn the condominium market around. Apparently, many politicians had invested in condominiums themselves and couldn't bear to see their investments falling apart. The laws that were passed generally gave condo associations the right to collect a certain amount of back condo fees during a foreclosure transaction. Therefore, if a bank foreclosed on a condominium, they had to fork over a statutory amount of back condo fees to the association. They had to do this whether or not the sale generated enough money to satisfy the original amount of the mortgage.

Then what happened? People again saw condominiums as stable investments, the condo market exploded, and everybody lived happily ever after, right?

No! When it comes to investing their money, most people are scared rabbits. They're just gonna follow the bunny trail, and if nobody's buyin' condos—new laws or not—they ain't buying condos. Period!

But you don't care, right? After all, you wanted a book on identity changing, not real estate economy. What the hell's the point anyway?

The point is that the 1990s became a boon to those of us in need of anonymous home ownership. Think about it. Failed condo associations looking to re-establish themselves under the protection of new laws. Banks looking to get out from under bad condo deals. Bank-owned condos averaging $20,000 per two-bedroom unit in not-so-bad locations. On top of all this, buyers are still scared to death of the condo market. Most of them never even heard of the new laws that protect associations. In fact, when I told my attorney that I was planning to invest in bank-owned condominiums, he advised me against it. To this day, I am grateful that I didn't listen to him!

If you don't mind doing your own property research, a bank will be happy to sell you a condo for cash and close the deal within two weeks of the initial offer. Their attorney will handle the whole closing at no extra charge, and the closing is so brief and informal you'll wonder if you really bought anything.

INTRO TO TRUSTS

This is "Intro to Trusts," or Trusts 101. Trusts will be covered in detail in the following chapter under the heading "Advanced Trusts" (i.e., Trusts 102). We are introducing the subject here because it can be relative to purchasing property. However, don't fear if a lot of the following information seems vague. Details will be filled in as we explore trusts further in the following chapter.

The ultimate in anonymity is to purchase a condo in a state where it is legal to place real estate assets in a trust with undisclosed beneficiaries. This type of transaction is perfectly legal in many states. Since this type of trust is commonly known as a business trust, the technical aspects will also be covered in the following chapter.

In a trust with undisclosed beneficiaries, a statement called the Schedule of Beneficiaries is filed with the trustee. As its title implies, the schedule of beneficiaries lists the beneficiaries of the trust. In some states, this paper does not need to be filed with the registrar of deeds. This is what you want.

There are also some states that distinguish a regular trust agreement from a real estate trust agreement. In these states, a trust where real estate is the only asset is known as a land trust. This type of trust is only permitted in a few states. If your state does not permit land trusts, then you will want to establish a standard business trust in which you will place personal property as well as real property.

At this point you're probably asking, "Who should be the trustee?" This is a good question. In most cases it will be your new identity, in one capacity or another, who signs the papers at the closing of the real estate transaction. This does not mean that your new identity has to act as trustee.

To take anonymity a step further, it would be nice to have a corporation act as trustee of your trust. Your new identity could now be acting as an officer of the corporation. Chapter 5 will deal with forming corporations in the "Establishing Business Entities" section. The advantage of having a corporation act as trustee is that your identity will not be placed in an index at the registry of deeds.

PUTTING IT ALL TOGETHER

Mixing all of the above ingredients, you can create the perfect hideout for yourself. Here is a step-by-step process that I have followed successfully. You will want to check the applicable laws of your target state before attempting this.

- Contact a Realtor and say you are interested in purchasing a bank-owned condo cheaply and quickly. Be sure to use your assumed identity.
- When you find a condominium that you like, make a cash offer that is 30 percent less than the bank's asking price and promise a fast closing. Banks like cash, and they will be anxious to get the white elephant off their books.
- The bank will counteroffer with a price $500–$1,000 higher than your offer. Accept this offer.
- At this point, the real estate agent will put you in touch with the bank's attorney. Tell her that the property will actually be deeded into a trust and that you will furnish her with a copy of the trust at the closing. At this point, the attorney will need the name of the trust as well as the name of the trustee (which could be a corporation) in order to prepare the title. Have this information ready. You may call the trust anything you like. Many people simply name the trust after the address of the property such as 123 Easy Street Trust. The trustee is the person who must appear at the closing.

To make things less complicated, it is best to have the trust set up and recorded with the county prior to the closing.

ESTABLISHING A PROFESSIONAL RESIDENCE

By establishing a professional residence such as a law office, doctor's office, or real estate agency, the identity changer effectively kills two birds with one stone. Once a professional residence is established, you will have a residence as well as a business address. It is not illegal for a non-attorney to set up a law office, nor is it illegal for a non-doctor to set up a doctor's office. As long as you don't take on clients or patients, you are not breaking the law.

Keep a separate business telephone line, and your credit applications will look very appealing. In fact, once you become part of a doctor or attorney mailing list, the creditors will seek you out.

You may also wish to maintain a separate business address to make things look even more legitimate. For instance, if you happen to set up your professional residence at 321 Quackery Lane, you may want to use 321 for your office address and R321 for your residential address. The "R" is usually accepted to mean "rear," as in rear of the building. You can think of it as meaning "residence" so that you'll never mix up your addresses. Usually such an address is written as 321R, but if you put the "R" first, the address will look that much more distinct to the credit bureau's computers.

Intimidation Factor

By being known as a professional and behaving in that manner, you will gain instant respect from loan officers, bureaucrats, and almost anybody you meet. It's much easier to pass your new identity off to someone if they're afraid to ask you questions and risk insulting you.

If you are lacking in verbal skills, you may want to brush up on your grammar and word power. Professionals such as doctors and attorneys are typically armed with powerful vocabularies and a professional, well-spoken manner. If you are lacking in either of these areas, people may not believe that you are a professional anything, much less a doctor or lawyer. Once somebody questions this, your whole identity will come into question.

There are several books and tapes dedicated to helping people improve their vocabulary, speaking skills, and memory (memory is linked to vocabulary). Local libraries will either have these materials or be able to direct you to someplace that does. So, did you get your library card yet?

PART TWO: TELEPHONES

A telephone number goes hand in hand with an established residence. So much so that, in reality, there are few people who have one without the other. (Anytime a bureaucrat asks for your address, the next question will inevitably be, "telephone number?")

A telephone number billed to your new identity at your new address is very appealing to banks, creditors, employers, and other parties hoping to form business relationships with you. Many lending institutions, including credit card companies, will actually score your credit application a point or two higher if you have a telephone in your own name that is billed to your address of record. (A person who is responsible enough to maintain his own telephone number is deemed more likely to take responsibility for his debts.) A typical point-scoring system for lenders and employers may look like this:

No telephone: 0 Points
Telephone in own name: 1 Point
Telephone billed to residence: 2 Points

The theory is that there are very few people who would go through this amount of trouble to obscure their true identity. Lending institutions are concerned that people who obscure their identity are more apt to skip out on payments or commit an outright fraud.

ESTABLISHING TELEPHONE SERVICE

If you have an actual residence under a new identity, it is a simple matter to order phone service. In most cases, all you need to tell the phone company is your name, address, and

Social Security Number. Be forewarned that the Social Security Number you give may be compared to the Social Security Death Index discussed in Chapter 3. This security check is a recent implementation by some telephone companies.

I recently tested this out with Nynex Telecommunications. I called Nynex to order some telephone service for a certain identity. I used the name, address, and Social Security Number of a person whom I knew to be deceased. The entire ordering process went smoothly until the end. The last thing the salesperson asked for was "my" Social Security Number. I gave her the one I knew to be retired and currently residing in the SSDI. The salesperson then placed me on hold, presumably to "get me a number." When she returned she said, "Sorry sir, but I can't give you a number today." When I inquired as to why, she said, "There are no numbers available for your area at the moment." This is an interesting response considering the fact that two entirely new exchanges had opened up in recent years. She suggested that I "call back on Monday." Right.

The point is to keep this example in mind when you are building your new identity. If you want your own phone number and the local phone company has this type of security check, make sure you find yourself a clean SSN!

RINGMATE LINES

A few years back, telephone companies began offering a service whereby more than one phone number can ring at the same line and be billed on the same bill. Each phone number has a distinct ring pattern. The service was originally marketed to households that had teenagers who received lots of calls. The idea is that you can give your teenager his or her own number for their friends to call. When the call comes through for the teen, the parents can identify it by the distinct ring pattern and not be troubled to answer the phone.

It didn't take long for home-based businesses to catch on to this idea. On one bill they could have a home phone, business line, and fax line. The additional RingMate lines usually cost about $3 each as opposed to $30 for a separate service.

The identity changer may wish to keep this wonderful service in mind when setting up a professional residence as described previously in this chapter. Certainly, if you use your noggin, you could dream up other convenient uses for this service.

VOICE MAIL

Once only available to large companies with big UNIX based computer systems in the basement, voice mail is now available to any schmuck with a PC, fax/modem/voice card, and the appropriate software.

A computer set up in your bedroom could answer the phone in the following manner:

Hello. You've reached Flimflam Enterprises. All associates are either away from their desks, on the phone, or busy assisting other customers. If you know your party's mailbox number, you may dial it at any time. If you'd like to leave a message for Zigfreid Flimflam, dial 201. If you'd like to leave a message for Yolanda Flimflam, dial 319. If you'd like a current stock quote, dial 999. To leave a message in the general message area, dial 0 or press *80 to begin sending your fax. Have a nice day.

Actually, most modern voice mail systems will receive a fax automatically, but if you want to sound big and important . . . well, you get the idea.

There are also devices sold by telephone companies and on the open market that will detect the ring pattern of a RingMate line and direct the call to the appropriate device or answering machine. In this way, you can direct your business line to your computer for fax and voice mail services and direct your residential line to an answering machine for a more "homey" greeting.

There is no rule restricting you to only one RingMate line. I know that most phone companies have deals where you can get two RingMate lines for $5. Most ring detectors are also designed to handle more than two rings. So, if you have two businesses, or if you want to give bill collectors a different phone number, or if you want a different phone number for people connected with your past life, you have many options available to you.

CALLER ID

A hotly debated privacy issue, but it looks like this one is here to stay. Caller ID is great for identity changers or other folks who may be leery about answering the phone and would like to know who's on the other end before picking up the line.

Another great feature is that you can log all calls placed to your residence even when you're not home. If you see any numbers that look suspicious, you can do reverse number searches through any of several databases available on CD-ROM for a PC. Or, if you don't have a PC (or just like to hate them), you can use a criss-cross directory such as those published by Cole Publications. These directories are very expensive, but if you go into any real estate office pretending to be a Realtor from a nearby office, they will usually let you use theirs.

Telephone companies as well as private concerns offer a myriad of Caller ID products for your perusal. If you are being hounded by creditors, a good Caller ID device called The Bouncer is available through Hello Direct. This device allows you to program in certain numbers or area codes that you do not want to deal with. When a person calls from that number or area code, the device "bounces" them out into TelCo limbo. The device will also bounce all calls that have their Caller ID "blocked" if you choose to set this option (blocking Caller ID is a favorite trick of bill collectors and investigators).

VOICE CHANGERS

Among the many other goodies available from telephone companies and third parties is the voice changer. A voice changer is a device that can make a man sound like a woman by raising the pitch of his voice or make a woman sound like a man by lowering the pitch. These devices are great for answering the phone in a small business. A man could answer the phone with the voice changer engaged acting as the secretary of the office. When the client on the other end then asks for the big boss, he can place the client on hold, switch the voice changer off, and pick up the phone again in an authoritative manner.

An obvious adaptation of this scheme could be used to avoid bill collectors. If a bill collector is looking for a man, answer the phone as a woman and your act will be all the more convincing.

If a potential employer is calling your "business" to verify past employment, you do not want to answer the phone with the same voice the employer just heard during your interview. Another use of the voice changer is born.

By the way, if you should ever screw up and answer the phone with the voice changer unknowingly disengaged, your client may say, "Gee, you and your boss sound a lot alike." If this happens, without becoming embarrassed or missing a beat simply state, "You know, everybody tells me that!" and continue about your business.

ANSWERING SERVICES

Answering services are good in a pinch for some business uses, but they are more costly than most other methods, and you never know who is answering the phone for you—sometimes the employees are rude to your callers. Answering services are also a turn-off to many people, and most people know when they've reached one.

For these reasons, employ answering services sparingly and judiciously, if at all.

SUMMARY

Much of the information presented in this chapter is linked to or can be used in close conjunction with the ideas to be presented in the next chapter. Residence, telephone service, employment, and education are at the heart of what society considers to be an established identity. By keeping this concept in mind as you read Chapter 5, you will better be able to create that image society is expecting.

CHAPTER FIVE

Education and Employment

For some reason, education and employment always seem to be intertwined. Personally, I've known a lot of MBAs who couldn't run a vacuum cleaner, much less a business. Likewise, I've known a few college slouches who've started bang-up companies. Nevertheless, the system expects that you will be educated in a certain way and that you will then obtain employment based on how many dates you had in college—or something like that.

Regardless of why they are intertwined, you, as an identity changer, will need to know how to obtain education and employment (or reasonable facsimiles thereof).

PART ONE: EDUCATION

From early childhood, we are taught that education is the key to finding a good job, and a good job is the key to providing for a family, and having a family is the key to happiness. Has anybody bothered to look at the latest divorce statistics?

One thing, at least, is true. Employment is often associated with education. In fact, most people's entire lives are centered around these two facets of existence. At an early age we are pushed into the education stream and told that our goal is to acquire sufficient knowledge so that we may eventually obtain a "good job" and have a means to provide for our own survival and perhaps even support a family.

Since these tenets are so ingrained in our society, the identity changer can expect to encounter some special problems relating to them. Some solutions to these problems are presented below.

COLLEGE CREDIT

Instead of attending on-campus classes, there are some really great alternatives to obtaining a college degree. In recent years, a subtle doctrine has begun creeping into our learning institutions. That doctrine is the idea that education takes place in the mind and not in the classroom; that it is the student who is responsible for his or her education and not the institution. Of course, many of the older, larger, and more established institutions of higher education vehemently oppose this radical heresy. Nonetheless, more and more schools are recognizing and granting credit for off-campus study. A good book on this subject is *College Degrees by Mail* by John Bear, published by Ten Speed Press in Berkeley, California.

One of the best legitimate off-campus colleges is Regent's College, which is part of the University of the State of New York and whose central office is located in Albany. There are various ways that credit can be earned at Regent's and similar colleges. A few sources of credit are:

- Transfer of college credits (not really an option for the identity changer)
- College-Level Proficiency Examinations (CLEP, ACTPEP, and advance placement)
- Portfolio-based assessments
- Telecourses
- Correspondence courses
- Independent study
- Courses offered by community colleges

The main problem with attending college under a new identity is getting credit for courses you've already taken. Obviously, you can't walk into the admissions department and say, "Oh, by the way, I've already earned an associate's degree under my previous identity." Unless you happen to work at a college and have the ability to do some mucking about in its computer systems, receiving credit for your previous education will have to be obtained, for a small fee, via advance placement or CLEP examinations. If you were one of those people who "crammed" just to pass the tests and never bothered to remember any of the material, you will find yourself learning it all over again.

PART TWO: EMPLOYMENT

By establishing a business entity, the identity changer can appear to own, be associated with, or be employed by a business.

Establishing a business entity could be useful during job hunts when a potential employer is seeking a business reference. Naturally, an identity changer does not want to use past jobs associated with his prior identity as references. This presents a problem. Although you may be qualified to do a certain job, there is nobody who will verify your past employment history. This is the same situation you were in when you first joined the work force. The difference is that everybody expects a 17-year-old kid to be looking for experience and a first job. Most of you reading this book look much older than 17, and any potential employer is going to expect that you've already established some work history for yourself. This is one reason why the identity changer needs to establish a business entity.

Aside from the reasons above, being associated with a business either as an owner or an employee has other advantages. For instance, maybe you don't even need a job. Maybe you're independently wealthy and desire to change your identity in order to avoid those nasty quarterly tax payments. Or perhaps you need to escape that ever-extending list of relatives who come sprawling and crawling, looking to sink their tiny, undeserving stubs into your hard-earned dough. In any case, if you've no need for a job, you may have considered skipping this chapter.

Before you skip ahead, though, read on a bit. Even if you don't need gainful employment, learning how to create the illusion of having it will prove useful to you in your identity-changing endeavors. Remember, the goal of an alternate identity is to create the impression that you are a hardworking, upstanding citizen ready to participate in the social betterment of your community. Therefore, appearing to be employed, whether or not you actually are, can only serve you in this regard.

TYPES OF BUSINESS ENTITIES

Business entities can take the following forms:

- Sole Proprietorship
- Partnership
  > Limited Partnership
  > Family Limited Partnership
- Corporation
  > For Profit Corporation
  > Nonprofit Corporation
- Business Trust

Each of these entities has its own advantages as well as disadvantages. The advantages are inherent to the entity itself but also contain a subset of ramifications for the identity changer. Thus, we will not only explore the traditional advantages and disadvantages of the various forms, but we will also discuss the special advantages and disadvantages as they pertain to identity changing.

Sole Proprietorship

A sole proprietorship is a business that is owned by an individual. The individual is personally liable for the income taxes and debts of the business. The individual may conduct business under his or her own name or under a fictitious name. If a sole proprietorship is to be conducted under a name other than the owner's real name, then the owner must file a "fictitious name statement" in the city or town where the business is located. This statement it typically referred to as a "DBA," which stands for "doing business as." A typical DBA statement would have the heading, "Theodore Thumbless D/B/A Fireworks R Us."

This statement puts the public on notice that the owner is conducting business under a name other than his real name. Also, all inquiries, comments, complaints, and service of process regarding said business may ultimately be directed to or served upon the owner of record.

The advantage of the sole proprietorship is its ease of start-up and lack of red tape. The disadvantage is that the person who starts the business must accept full liability for all claims brought against the business. Therefore, if the business is sued and it does not have enough assets to pay the court settlement, the plaintiff can look to the owner's personal assets and estate to collect the judgment.

Sole proprietorships have limited use to the identity changer. Typical uses would be mail anonymity and free magazine subscriptions. I suppose that a DBA could be used as supporting evidence for identity when opening bank accounts, although I've never found this necessary. In any case, the town clerk will ask you for identification when you fill out the DBA.

Partnerships

A partnership, as its name implies, is a business entity established by two or more individuals known as partners. This arrangement is often referred to as a general partnership.

Unless otherwise agreed upon, partnerships formed by two individuals will give each individual a 50 percent share in the business as well as 50 percent of the voting power. Similarly, a partnership formed by three individuals will give each partner a one-third share and voting interest in the business. Most states recognize this default partnership status unless a contract between the partners specifically calls for a different arrangement.

The partnership is somewhat more of an entity unto itself

than is the sole proprietorship. The partners must vote and decide on business matters, but each partner is still ultimately responsible for the taxes and debts of his share of the business. This means that creditors may look to the individual partners to satisfy debts if the partnership itself becomes insolvent. There must be a better way . . .

Limited Partnerships

The limited partnership is a statutory device allowing third parties, sometimes called "silent partners," to invest in a partnership with limited liability. Generally speaking, a limited partner is only liable to the partnership to the extent of his investment. In other words, if a limited partner invests $50,000 in a business and the business becomes insolvent, the limited partner can only lose $50,000. A limited partner cannot have his personal assets attached to satisfy claims against the partnership.

Limited partnerships are controlled by statute. In most states the statute is based, in whole or in part, on the Uniform Limited Partnership Act. There are certain requirements that must be met in order for the limited partnership to be valid. The main requirements are:

- An agreement, usually referred to as a Certificate of Limited Partnership, must be in writing and filed with the appropriate state agency (usually, the recorder's office in the county where the partnership is located, or the Secretary of State's office). This agreement in itself must also meet certain statutory requirements in order to be valid.
- Limited partners may not have control over the business.
- Limited partners may not include their name in the title of the partnership.

A good book on this subject and asset protection in general is *Lawsuit and Asset Protection* by Vijay Fadia and published by Homestead Publishing Company, Incorporated. For a wonderful education, you may wish to write them at 21707

Hawthorne Boulevard, Suite 204, Torrance, CA 90503, and order a copy.

A limited partnership offers certain advantages to the identity changer. Several paper identities can be set up as limited partners. In turn, these partners can hold assets for you in the event your main identity (general partner) gets into any legal trouble.

The limited partnership can file for a Tax Identification Number from the IRS (form SS4) and open one or more bank accounts. There is no need to give the bank any Social Security Number!

The limited partnership can also hire employees and give them W2 forms or 1099 forms at the end of the year. This places identities (and their Social Security Numbers) in the government's computers.

Although creditors cannot legally take a partner's interest to satisfy the partner's personal debts, a court may grant the creditor a "charging order" to attach the debtor partner's interest in the partnership. Creditors generally steer clear of trying to obtain charging orders. Unless unusually large sums of money are involved, it is not economically feasible for creditors to do so.

Additionally, a savvy debtor can maintain full control of his assets by making himself the general partner of the partnership with an ownership interest of 5 percent and a controlling interest of 100 percent. If the partnership happens to make a profit in any given quarter, the general partner can elect to *not* distribute dividends. Even if a creditor takes the time and is lucky enough to get a charging order against the general partner's 5 percent interest in the partnership, he cannot collect on undistributed income. Moreover, the creditor now owns the general partner's tax position on the undistributed income. The general partner is obligated to send the creditor an IRS K-1 form declaring his undistributed gain and the creditor is obliged to pay tax on it! As you can see, it is not in the creditor's best interest to pursue charging orders against a debtor's share of a limited partnership.

Corporations

Once formed, a corporation is an entity unto itself. It is owned by shareholders and controlled by a board of directors. The corporation may file for a Tax Identification Number, open bank accounts, conduct business, file lawsuits, and be sued in the name of the corporation. The formation, control, and operation of corporations are governed by statutes and regulations, which differ from state to state.

One disadvantage of the corporation is that the various states require a filing fee upon its establishment and also require annual reports to be filed. The filing of the annual report may also involve a fee. Another disadvantage is the corporation's susceptibility to double taxation. The corporation, as an entity unto itself, is taxed, and then the shareholders, upon receiving dividends, are taxed again. However, certain small corporations may avoid this double taxation by filing as "S" corporations.

The advantages of a corporation, as distinguished from a limited partnership or business trust (described below), are:

- Legal in every state
- Esteem associated with the word "corporate"
- Business form is readily accepted by government and general public

The main advantage of a corporation, however, is that the shareholders are shielded from personal liability in suits brought against the corporation.

The big benefit to the identity changer is that the corporation can have a bank account in its own name with its own tax ID number. This is a better alternative to playing the Social Security game with the feds. It's much safer and, if done right, perfectly legal. However, unless you keep large sums of money on deposit, bank accounts for corporations usually carry higher monthly fees, and account activity is assessed a per-check and/or per-deposit surcharge. However, for the safety and peace of mind achieved, it is well worth it.

Nevada/Delaware Corporations

So what's all this hype about Nevada and Delaware corporations, anyway? Incorporating in these two states is thought to have certain advantages to those of us interested in privacy. This is true to an extent; however, many of the claims made by "incorporating services" in these states also hold true in many other states. Typical claims include:

- Shareholders are not a matter of public record
- One person may hold all officer and director positions
- No minimum corporate bank account
- No income tax
- Incorporators do not have to visit or reside in the state
- Ability to incorporate by phone or mail

All these conveniences are fine and dandy, but many other states offer some or all of these same "advantages." Without going into a lot of detail about Nevada and Delaware corporations, I will tell you that their two best features are:

- One person may hold all officer and director positions
- No income tax

Although other states may have these advantages, many of the more densely populated states do not. Certainly, it is a great advantage to the identity changer if he or she can hold all officer and director positions. This eliminates the need to forge extra signatures or seek out conspirators.

The state of Nevada is virtually tax free. It does have a Nevada business tax, but organizations without employees are exempt from paying it. If, for some reason, you do wish to declare employees in Nevada, the tax is $25 per employee, per year. There are no other taxes that the corporation needs to worry about. A smart businessperson might use the Nevada corporation as a wholesaler, distributor, leasing agent, lending institution, advertising agent, management company, and home office for all invoices to avoid taxes and move income to a tax-free state.

TRUSTS

Often enigmatic, even to the people who use them, trusts can be understood if you take the time to examine their varied uses. Perhaps one reason why trusts are so mysterious is because there are several types, and most people don't understand their differences. In fact, most do not know that there *are* any differences.

The various forms of trusts are:

- Living
- Testamentary
- Revocable
- Irrevocable
- Land
- Realty
- Business

Don't skip ahead yet! I'm not going to burden you with detailed explanations of all these variations. Most of them are useless to the identity changer anyway. I merely list them here for the sake of completeness and for your own future reference.

Briefly, the first four trusts—living, testamentary, revocable, and irrevocable—are used primarily for estate planning, which is beyond the scope of this book. Land and realty trusts are essentially the same thing and may or may not have any distinction from any other trust, depending on what state you're in. This leaves the business trust. The business trust may be very useful to the identity changer, indeed.

Basic Form of a Trust

The basic form of any type of trust agreement is essentially the same. The main parts are:

- *Trustor*. The person who creates the trust by transferring property to the trustee.

- *Trustee.* The person who "cares for" the trust property.
- *Beneficiaries.* The people who have actual ownership interest in the trust property.

One person may be trustor, trustee, and beneficiary simultaneously. However, courts in most jurisdictions will dissolve such a trust to satisfy judgment creditors of the trustor.

Business Trust

A business trust, sometimes called a Common Law Trust, is a little-known form of business organization still perfectly legal in many states. Many years ago, investors in Massachusetts were not permitted to form corporations for the purpose of real estate acquisition and development. The Massachusetts Business Trust was born out of efforts by investors to circumvent statutes regulating corporations. The investors wanted to create a device whereby they could protect themselves from personal liability in the real estate business. Trusts were formed as an alternative, and their structure was upheld by courts and common law without the necessity of enacting statutes.

Trustee: A Trustee sits on the Board of Trustees and votes on matters before the Trust, much like a director in a corporation.

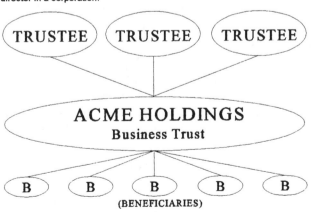

Business Trust: A stand-alone entity, just like a person, that can conduct business, hold title to property, maintain bank accounts and assert or defend itself in civil court actions. Persons having claims or judgments against the Trust may only look to the Trust Property for payment.

Beneficiaries: A Beneficiary is a person who owns shares of the Trust and thus has a Beneficial Interest in the Trust Property. A Beneficiary has no control over the Trust other than to elect Trustees.

Courts have also upheld that the formation and use of business trusts is not limited to real estate investing. In this regard, the Massachusetts Business Trust became a common law device whereby a business could be formed, limiting liability to its shareholders (beneficiaries of the trust), and avoiding the taxes, fees, and regulation of the corporate structure.

As you may have already guessed, the IRS has enacted laws to make sure that these entities are taxed as corporations, and courts in several states have failed to recognize the Massachusetts Business Trust as a vehicle to limit investor liability. Some states, most notably Washington, fail to recognize business trusts altogether.

The good news is that there are still many states that continue to recognize the business trust, now often referred to as the "common law trust," as a completely valid business entity. Among these states are California, Illinois, Maryland, Massachusetts, Michigan, New Jersey, New York, Pennsylvania, West Virginia, and Wisconsin. A few states have even enacted statutes to protect this form of business organization. Massachusetts, of course, is one such state. California and Wisconsin are two others.

Arizona, Indiana, Kansas, Kentucky, Louisiana, and Texas have all adopted special rules for dealing with business trusts. If you're looking to set up in one of these states, you will want to review the laws and case histories of that particular state.

In Arkansas, California, Illinois, Massachusetts, Missouri, New York, and Rhode Island, beneficiaries who retain little or no control over the operation of a business trust will, in most circumstances, be exempt from personal liability to the trust.

A business trust, like any other form of business entity, may apply for a Tax Identification Number, open a bank account, and conduct business in the name of the trust. They can be a great advantage to the identity changer because ownership of real, personal, and business property can be held anonymously in trust, with the identity changer, or third party, acting as trustee. If you exercise a certain amount of cunning as an identity changer, you can convince a bank, trust institution, or attorney to act as trustee for your trust. Your name will never appear anywhere in public record. Thus, creditors and investigators of your current or past identity will have no way of knowing that you have any assets to attach, nor will your name be gratuitously supplied to the various databases that we have discussed throughout this book.

FILLING OUT FORM SS-4

Form SS-4 is the IRS form a business entity uses to apply for an Employer Identification Number (EIN), also commonly referred to as a Taxpayer Identification Number. The EIN is the business entity's equivalent to a Social Security Number, and it is the number that banks and creditors will require of you when transacting business. Any form of business organization, including a sole proprietorship, may apply for an EIN.

The IRS requires the person filling out Form SS-4 to furnish their Social Security Number for the IRS records. Do not worry too much about this part. This is only a precautionary measure taken by the IRS. Be sure to use the techniques from Chapter 3 to furnish them with a valid SSN, just for good measure. As long as your business never gets into any trouble, the IRS has no need to check out the Social Security Number that you give them. It will not become a matter of public record, and creditors will never find it in any database.

PLAYING THE PART

When you are purporting to be a business, whether a sole proprietorship, partnership corporation, or trust, it is not only important that you meet all of the statutory filing requirements, but you must also carry out the business as a business truly would. This means that you must file for your Tax Identification Number as soon as the business is established. You must pay business bills out of the business account and personal bills out of your personal account (or, at least, appear to do so). You must pay employees if the business claims to have them, file tax returns, and make payments toward loans or mortgages that your business claims to be liable for.

This is important because investigators for the IRS, bankruptcy trustees, and creditors look for this kind of consistent behavior when investigating you or doing business with you. Additionally, courts will look for this type of consistent business behavior when investigating creditor claims that the business was a sham or a fraud. In short, if you say you're a business, act like a business. This is the best protection you could ever have.

JOB FRONTS

Even if you don't have the desire or ambition to use business entities for your own anonymity or asset-protection purposes, as an identity changer you will need references when seeking employment elsewhere. Here is a quick outline to accomplish just that.

- Decide upon a business entity with which you would like to be associated.
- Establish a name, address, and phone number for that business.
- Go on your job interviews late in the day so you can be in the "office" with your voice changer (see Chapter 4) the next day when the potential employer calls to verify your previous "experience."
- When the employer calls the next day to check your references, have your "secretary" verify your excellent work history.

Incidentally, some answering services will answer your line any way you like and regurgitate anything you tell them to.

This is yet another alternative, but it is not nearly as impressive as the method outlined above. People can tell when they have reached an answering service!

SELF-EMPLOYMENT:
THE ROAD TO TRUE PERSONAL FREEDOM

Being self-employed and an entrepreneur at heart, it's difficult for me to not let my bias on this issue enter into this book. The question is, if you're not working for yourself, then who are you working for?

Think about how society is fed to us and the things that led you to read this book. Corporate America has an ingenious way of keeping the masses busy. An entry-level job in a corporation typically yields the young college grad somewhere between $20,000 to $30,000 per year. The corporate debutant is rather pleased with earning this salary. He'll casually slip it in at social gatherings, e.g., "Well, my wife and I discussed it and we had decided to hold out for twenty-five, but during my last interview the senior executive mentioned that the benefits were quite extensive, so I settled for twenty-four." The "thousand" is always implied in these conversations.

At the time of his first "real" job offer, the debutant resides in a modest apartment with his wife, and the new job can mean only one thing: it's time to buy a "home." Well, any good citizen knows that you simply can't go out, purchase a house, and live in it. First you must be prequalified, which is an interesting practice. Prequalification is a way for Corporate America to determine exactly how much money it can suck out of you without causing you to become insolvent. At the end of prequalification, the applicant is told he should be buying a home in the $130,000 to $140,000 price range. Ninety-nine percent of all junior corporate members blindly follow the home-buying process, from prequalification to closing. When it's all over, they wonder why they are struggling to keep up with payments, property maintenance, job requirements, and social life.

This struggling to keep up with everything is really just a way to keep you busy until you die. Corporations like to keep the masses concerned with things such as weight, appearance, health, social status, and, most of all, net worth. (I have heard people ask, "I wonder what my net worth is?" I would suggest that a person's "net worth" is very low if they think that it can be measured in terms of dollars.) In this way, Corporate America ensures that you will have no initiative of your own, whatsoever, outside of keeping up with Mr. Jones next door.

You see, corporations don't want people getting ideas of their own and becoming the competition. Government does not want people getting together and becoming politically active. Everything must remain static. The status quo must be preserved so that those who are munching on a big piece of pie may continue munching on that pie. The masses must be led to believe that the leftover crumbs are magnanimous profferings from above and are more than enough to sustain them.

This is not to say the corporate route should be totally eliminated. If you are to gain true personal freedom, however, climbing the corporate ladder should be a means to an end. In essence, you should use the corporation as a path to your ultimate goal instead of letting the corporation use you.

If you opt to not work for yourself but use the corporation to obtain your personal goals, you may be met with two seemingly impenetrable barriers—education and experience. Past work experience can be "obtained" by using the job front methods outlined above. And there are a couple of ways around the education problem.

If you are extremely knowledgeable in your profession and can readily demonstrate this, many corporations may not care if you hold an actual degree. Case in point: Bill Gates, cofounder and largest shareholder of Microsoft Corporation. In case you make your home immediately below a large moss-bearing rock, I'll tell you that Microsoft Corporation has the distinction of owning the rights to the operating system in almost every IBM-compatible personal computer sold in today's market. It seems that some years ago, while Mr. Gates was attending Harvard, he became aware of an opportunity in the computer industry. He dropped out of college to pursue this opportunity. Not long after that, IBM, anxious to get into the personal computer craze, was pursuing Bill Gates. Despite his apparent lack of college credentials, Mr. Gates entered into a contract with IBM and has since blown them out of the water, leaving them stuck with their bulky mainframes and forever locked out of the personal computer market.

So, if you have some special ability, don't be afraid to approach a corporation with an offer of your own. To protect your past identity, a little well-mannered attitude will go a long way. If questions arise, simply remind them that you have a special ability and you are wondering if your services will be needed. Beyond that, you're not willing to indulge them.

If you don't have enough confidence in your abilities to pull off the above approach, a little educational background would certainly aid you in your job search.

SUMMARY

This chapter is filled with a lot of legal and technical information with which any identity changer should become familiar. By having a better understanding of the legal, social, and economic foundations of the business community, the identity changer will gain an advantage when working and residing within that community.

If most of this information is new to you, I recommend you reread this chapter at a later date. When you are finally comfortable with all of the above topics, you can then research your state statutes and case histories at your local library. By doing this, you will become more knowledgeable than most businesspersons in your community. Armed with that knowledge, you will become more powerful and enjoy an advantageous position. Knowledge *is* power. Now, you can create or find meaningful employment for your new identity.

CHAPTER SIX

Making a Work ID

In this chapter we are going to focus on making an employment identification card. In making this ID, we will use a specific process that I have developed as a private detective. The exact tools and procedures can be used in the manufacture and duplication of other forms of identification. It is at your discretion to customize and amend these concepts to suit your own needs.

This method is the "School of Hard Knocks" approach to ID manufacture. You are encouraged to find more efficient methods of reproducing and eventually improving on the quality of the finished product. Even though I now own more sophisticated software and machinery, I still use this old, comfortable method. It has withstood the test of time.

PART ONE: PREPARATION

Before we begin the actual construction of our work ID, let's spend a little time discussing the tools, materials, and concepts involved. A little forethought and preparation will greatly enhance the final product.

REQUIRED TOOLS

• A personal computer with ink jet, bubble jet, or laser printer

- Windows Paintbrush software (usually comes with PC)
- Windows Write word processing software (usually comes with PC)
- A 35mm SLR camera with a macro lens for close-up photography
- Paper cutter
- Transparency sheets
- White or parchment bond paper
- Glue stick/glue pen
- Self-adhesive lamination sheets
- Clear piece of glass, 8″ x 10″ or larger

OPTIONAL TOOLS

- Camera tripod
- Laminating machine and lamination cards

WHAT TO INCLUDE ON AN EMPLOYMENT ID

You will want to include the following headings on the front of an employment ID: name, birth date, hire date, issue date, height, weight, color of eyes and hair, employee identification number, a security signature, your signature, a "validating" signature, and, in some cases, an expiration date.

The birth date is included in your employment ID to serve as a backup for the birth certificate that you will eventually obtain. For similar reasons, it is a good idea if your employee identification number also happens to match the Social Security Number you plan on using. The use of the SSN for such purposes is not considered out of the ordinary. Thus, using it in this manner could be to your advantage in many situations.

The reverse side of the ID should include address, phone number, and some other information specific to the company allegedly issuing the ID. This adds a touch of authenticity. Our ID will look like this:

Acme Security & Investigation Co.
Rochester Division
Employee:
Title or Position:
Employee ID#:
Usual Location:

Security Clearance Code:

Sex: DOB:
Height: Hire Date:
Weight: Issue Date:
Hair: Valid To:
Eyes: License No:

Employee's Signature   Validating Signature

SECURITY CLEARANCE CODES

1A	Highest access available. Twenty-four hour access to all locations. No electromagnetic screening necessary.
1B	Twenty-four hour access to "Usual Location" No screening necessary Satellite divisions: must have escort; 9-5 only.
2A	Independent Contractor. Standard screening
2B	New employee. Follow standard screening.
3	Standard screening at all times.

ACME Security & Investigation Co.
294 Washington Street
Rochester, NY 10011
(212) 555-1234

IDENTIFICATION MUST BE RETURNED UPON TERMINATION

Later you will use the above diagram to construct your own reverse side for your ID. Detailed instructions will not be given. When you are done making the front of the ID, you will have learned enough to construct the back without any problems. Be sure not to laminate before adding the reverse side!

85

A Word About Security Devices

In addition to the above headings, your ID will include a security signature and official seal, both of which will partly overlap the photograph. This procedure is often used in identity documents as a security measure. Many state licensing bureaus use it to prevent would-be forgers from placing their picture onto someone else's professional license or driver's license. By being aware of this type of security measure, police officers can catch unlicensed drivers, illegal immigrants, and underage drinkers who attempt to stick their picture on the license of another person. When the cop discovers half a signature sticking out from underneath the photograph of an altered ID, he will dismantle that particular work of art and have the bearer arrested.

Other bureaucrats are also privy to this type of security measure, which is precisely why we want to include it on our employment ID. The bureaucrat assumes that the average citizen would not know enough to doctor up an ID that includes such a sophisticated security device. Because of this, your innocent employment ID can become a very powerful tool in your effort to change your identity.

PART TWO: MAKING THE ID

This ID will be constructed in three layers. The first layer is a page containing the "ID body" with the personal information of the "employee" properly filled out.

The next layer is the photograph that will be placed in the upper-left corner of the ID body.

The final layer is a transparency sheet that will contain a security signature and official seal partly overlapping the photograph.

Once these three parts are aligned, we will keep them in place by laying a piece of clear glass over them. We will then photograph the assembly so that the final product is a one-piece unit that will be laminated for a professional-looking finished product.

～ •

PASSPORT PHOTOS

The first step in making any ID is to get a picture of yourself. It is not recommended that you use one of those booths that are found in amusement parks. We must remember to be professional. If your intention is to make an ID that is supposed to have been issued some years ago, be sure to use an older picture of yourself.

In most cities, you can walk into any camera shop and obtain a passport photo for $6 to $9. The whole process takes about five minutes. When you do this, be sure that you are clean shaven, of neat appearance, and have on a proper dress shirt. Of course, if the ultimate image you want to convey is that you are a poor working stiff and desperately in need of welfare and Social Security, you may want to amend this dress code accordingly.

Before the picture is snapped, it is best to look slightly up and to your left. This will produce a more regal appearance on the final product, and you will be looking in toward the center of the ID as opposed to the outer reaches of the galaxy or worse, directly at the camera. You are trying to avoid a mug shot or looking like a waste product. If your picture looks antisocial, bureaucrats will hone in on it, scrutinize you, judge you, sentence you to exile, and otherwise decline to do business with you.

If you are planning to use the passport photo to reproduce your state driver's license or some other specific document, be sure that you are sitting in front of the right color backdrop. To be safe, it is best to bring your own. Make sure it is one or two shades lighter than what you want for the final product. If the color is a shade of blue, you might want to lighten it by three to four shades, as whites and blues tend to get more blue when photographed. The person taking the picture may tell you that it's not what the passport office wants and that you really should use the studio's backdrop. If this happens, just tell them that the photo is not actually for a passport but that you and your sister are making up novelty IDs for your mother's sixtieth birthday. Tell them whatever you feel like; they won't care. All they want is your six dollars. They will only mention the color of the backdrop as a favor to you.

When you leave the camera store, you will have two 2″ by 2″ photographs.

TRIMMING TIPS AND TRICKS

Sometimes these passport photographs don't completely fill up the paper on which they are printed. For this ID, which will have the picture in the upper left corner, you will produce a better final product if the bottom and right edges of the photo do not have any excess print paper or border. For IDs where the picture will be in the center, you will produce a better final product if the photo has no border at all. If these edges are not clean, trim them with a paper cutter. Though there are two photos, it is possible that only one will need to be trimmed or that each one will need to be trimmed differently. Do not use scissors or a razor blade to trim the photo unless you have an extremely good eye and a surgeon's hand. Any curved or uneven edges will show through on the final product.

Here are some tips when using a paper cutter. For starters, don't "eyeball" your measurements. Use a ruler to draw a straight line along every edge you plan to cut. Draw the line so that it goes right off the surface that you are cutting. In this way, you can easily match the line up with the edge of the paper cutter. Another good trick is to use the paper cutter in a well-lit area. Kneel down beneath the paper cutter so that it is above eye level. You will then be able to see the light coming through the photograph (or whatever you happen to be cutting), and the edge you need to cut can then be aligned with the edge of the paper cutter. Use a lint-free paper towel or a clean sheet of paper to hold photographs. This will prevent fingerprints. When you have the object you are trimming properly aligned, you can then cut it.

Sometimes, the blade of the paper cutter causes the object

to bend or twist as you are cutting it. This is especially true if you are cutting something thick. A nice trick in this situation is to place the flat side of a pencil along the edge you will be cutting. Hold the pencil down firmly with the tips of your fingers while you are cutting the object. *Be careful and cut slowly!* Your fingers will be very close to the blade at this point, and you will have little space in which to maneuver them. So remember, hold firmly, keep fingers clear, cut slowly, and you will have no problem. You will get a nice, clean, straight cut.

BODY OF THE ID

The body of the ID is the front of the ID, which contains all the headings and has an area for the photograph. The personal information and picture are put in later. In essence, it is a blank ID card that can be filled in by anybody. Here are the actual steps used in making the body of the ID.

Power-up your PC, start Windows, and double click the Windows Paintbrush icon to start Paintbrush. Once Paintbrush is running, choose View and then Cursor Position from the menu bar. A little window will pop up at the top of your screen, indicating the horizontal and vertical location of the mouse cursor.

Drawing Boxes

From the tool box on the left of your screen, choose the "draw square" icon, which is the sixth icon, counting down, on the left-most side of your screen. From the line size box (immediately below the tool box), choose the thinnest line. This is the uppermost line.

Go to cursor location 25, 25, click and hold the mouse button down, and drag the mouse to cursor position 500, 360. Release the mouse button and you will have a big, black rectangle on your screen. This is the outline of the ID.

Now we are going to make another box where the picture will go. Move the mouse to cursor position 25, 25, click and hold the mouse button down, and drag the mouse to cursor position 205, 205. Release the mouse and you now have a space for your picture.

To draw the signature boxes at the bottom, move the mouse to position 25, 325, then click and drag to 500, 360. Move again to 25, 325, then click and drag to 262, 360. You now have two signature boxes.

Move to position 205, 170, click and drag to 500, 205, and you are done with box drawing for the day!

Making Headings

Now switch to the text tool. This is the icon depicting the letters ABC. Next, choose Text and then Fonts from the menu bar. Choose a nice font for your company name. In the example, I used a font called "Splendid." This font may not be available on your system. If not, simply choose another font that you like, then choose "regular" for the font style and choose 14 for "size." Press OK to get back to the drawing board.

Move to cursor position 220, 50, click the mouse, and type in a name for your company. You may have to choose a different starting position for the cursor to get your company name centered.

Now you must change fonts again for the subheading ("Rochester Division" in our example). Choose Text, Fonts, Arial font, bold font style, size 14. Move to cursor position 265, 75, click the mouse, and type in your subheading. Again, if your subheading is different than the one in our example, you may have to adjust the starting cursor position to get the subheading centered.

Now that you are getting the hang of things, here are the cursor positions and fonts for the remainder of the headings:

Arial, Bold, Size 12

Move to 215, 100, click mouse and type:
Employee:

Hit "enter" and type:
Title or Position:
Hit "enter" and type:
Employee ID#:
Hit "enter" and type:
Usual Location:

Move to 35, 225, click mouse and type:
Sex:
Hit "enter" and type:
Height:
Hit "enter" and type:
Weight:
Hit "enter" and type:
Hair:
Hit "enter" and type:
Eyes:

Move to 270, 225, click mouse and type:
DOB:
Hit "enter" and type:
Hire Date:
Hit "enter" and type:
Issue Date:
Hit "enter" and type:
Valid To:
Hit "enter" and type:
License No:

Arial, Regular, Size 14

Move to 245, 195 and type:
Security Clearance Code:

Arial, Regular, Size 8

Move to 30, 335, click mouse, and type:
Employee's Signature
Move to 268, 335, click mouse, and type:
Validating Signature

Select File, Save, and type file name: WORK_ID.BMP

You are done entering text for the day. Be sure to save your work! Now you may print out your ID body and marvel at it. Though the ID on the screen may look very large, rest assured that it will print out at approximately 3″ by 5″. At this point you may wish to fill out the ID card with the vital information of your identity. This can be done with a typewriter. If you don't have a typewriter, here is yet another trick.

Double click on the Windows Write icon to start the word processing software. When the program starts, the cursor will be in the upper left corner of the page. Choose Character, then Fonts, and select "Courier New" font, "Regular" font style, and size 14.

Press "enter" four times.

Press "tab" six times and enter the name you will be using. Press enter.

Press "tab" six times and enter your title or position. Press enter.

Press "tab" six times and enter your ID number. Press enter.

Press "tab" six times and enter your usual location. Press enter twice.

Tab over eight times, press space bar twice, and type in your security clearance code. Press enter.

Here are the tab locations for the remaining information. The tabs used are the same ones used in our example. However, if you change the length of some of the information, you may have to add or subtract a tab to get things to line up.

Tab once and type: Male
Tab 6 times and type: 1/1/60   Hit enter

Tab once and type: 6' 2"
Tab 5 times and type: 5/14/92   Hit enter
Tab once and type: 190lbs
Tab 5 times and type: 5/16/95   Hit enter
Tab once and type: Brown
Tab 5 times and type: 5/16/98   Hit enter
Tab once and type: Blue
Tab 6 times and type: SG-345

Notice how the tabs change depending on the length of the information entered. As you enter your own customized vital statistics, you will need to make adjustments.

One final adjustment is necessary. The information you typed in for your security clearance code (1B, in our example) must be brought to a larger font size so that everything lines up when we print this file onto the Paintbrush file.

To adjust the font size, highlight the 1B. Place the cursor just to the left of the 1, click the mouse, and drag it just to the right of the B. Now, 1B will be white with black background;

	Acme Security & Investigation Co.
	Rochester Division
	Employee: Mack Thuniphe
	Title or Position: Guard
	Employee ID#: 012-34-0000
	Usual Location: Rochester, NY
	Security Clearance Code: 1B

Sex: Male	**DOB:** 1/1/60
Height: 6' 2"	**Hire Date:** 5/14/92
Weight: 190lbs	**Issue Date:** 5/16/95
Hair: Brown	**Valid To:** 5/16/98
Eyes: Blue	**License No:** SG-345

Employee's Signature	Validating Signature

this is what highlighting is. Choose Character, then Fonts, and select size 18. Courier New and "Regular" will already be selected. Press OK.

To get the margins to line up with our WORK_ID.BMP file, choose Document, Page Layout from the menu bar. Enter 1.35" for the left margin and 1.1" for the top margin. Press OK.

Choose, File, Save, and type in file name: VTLSTATS.WRI

Believe it or not, the information in this file will line up with the headings in your Paintbrush file. Try it out! Print out your Paintbrush file, then refeed the paper into your printer, same side and same direction. Now print out the word processing file onto the same page. Go ahead, don't be shy. Now, is that a neat trick or what? See the illustration on page 93 to see how it should look.

If Things Don't Line Up

What if it looks like this:

	Acme Security & Investigation Co.
	Rochester Division Mack Thuhiphe
	Employee: Guard
	Title or Position: 012-34-0000
	Employee ID#: Rochester, NY
	Usual Location:
Male	**Security Clearance Code:** 1B 1/1/60
Sex: 6' 2"	**DOB:** 5/14/92
Height: 190lbs	**Hire Date:** 5/16/95
Weight: Brown	**Issue Date:** 5/16/98
Hair: Blue	**Valid To:** SG-345
Eyes:	**License No:**
Employee's Signature	Validating Signature

The previous example was printed on a Hewlett Packard Desk Jet 500 and a 500C without any problems. There are some printers, such as the HP Laser Jet III and Panasonic KX-P4420, that add a .25″ header to the Windows Write word processor file.

To compensate for this, Choose Document, Page Layout from the menu bar. Enter 1.35″ for the left margin and .85″ for the top margin (.25″ less than before). Press OK.

Obviously, I couldn't check out this technique on every possible printer, so some of you may have to find adjustments particular to your printer. One thing is certain, though: the spacing relationships between WORK_ID.BMP and VTLSTATS.WRI will always be the same. The worst case is that you'll have to play with the margins in VTLSTATS.WRI to get things to line up on your printer.

DESIGNING A SECURITY SIGNATURE

A security signature is a signature that will partially overlap the photograph just like you can find on many state driver's licenses. Our security signature will also bend around the bottom right corner of the photograph for an added touch of authenticity.

Some sophisticated word processors and graphics programs will allow you to rotate text, and these may come in handy if you don't mind using a "script" style font for your security signature. If you're computer literate enough to know how to use these programs, then you don't need any detailed explanations from me. So what follows is the poor man's method of bending computer-generated signatures.

First decide on a signature. The signature of an officer or similar authoritative person is preferable for most uses. Use of a first initial and middle name also provides a more official sounding title. Some suggestions:

• Colonel F. Winston Cahill

- General R. Scott Farrington
- G. William Bendt, CEO

The best way to divide the signature is to leave the last quarter to third bending up the right side of the photograph. In the above examples the names Cahill, Farrington, and the title CEO would be the vertical print in our finished product.

Here we will design a Windows Paintbrush file with a security signature and a cross-hair marker where you will paste your official seal for the transparency master. This file will line up directly with the ID file we have already created.

Open Windows Paintbrush. (By now you must be feeling like a pro with this program, right?) Select View, Cursor Position, so that you can see your screen coordinates.

From the menu bar choose Text and from the text dialog box choose Fonts. Select the "Script" font and choose "Regular" font style, size 18. Choose the ABC tool right beneath the scissors icon on the left side of your screen.

Move the cursor to coordinates 70, 210.

Type: *Colonel H. William.*

Move the cursor to coordinates 670, 210. To do this, you will need to "scroll" the screen to the right by pressing on the right-facing scroll arrow at the bottom of the screen (located immediately above the light-brown color block).

Type: *Farrington.*

Now scroll back all the way to the left margin. Select the line-drawing tool located immediately beneath the paintbrush icon. Choose the thinnest line setting.

Move to cursor position 206, 35, click the mouse, and drag it down to position 206, 65 to draw the vertical line of the cross hair.

Move to cursor position 190, 50, click the mouse, and drag

it down to position 222, 50 to draw the horizontal line of the cross hair.

Here's what your file should look like at this point:

Now, print off a copy of the ID file that we made, WORK_ID.BMP. When that is done printing, refeed the paper back into the printer, same side, same direction, and print off a copy of the transparency file, SIG&SEAL. BMP. Make sure you are printing in "Portrait Printing" mode. Then, when that is done, refeed the paper back into the printer, same side, reverse direction. Choose File, Print Setup, check off the "Landscape Printing" box, and click OK. Print the transparency file onto the page again. How do things line up? See the illustration on page 98 to see how it should look.

Now is that a neat trick or what? Yes, the two halves of the signature do print out elsewhere on the page, but this will not interfere with your 3″ by 5″ ID. Though we used Windows Paintbrush as an example, you could easily adapt this technique to other paint programs if you desire.

DESIGNING
AN OFFICIAL SEAL

Official seals can be found all over the place and come in a variety of shapes and sizes. The three most popular shapes are

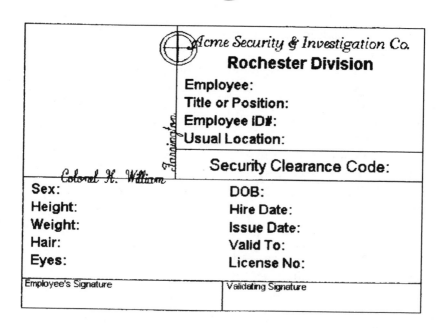

the circle, shield, and badge. Some examples are illustrated on the following page.

Most official federal, state, city, and corporate documents that you come across can provide you with a nice example of an official seal. If you have trouble finding any examples of seals, simply write to your secretary of state's office in regards to any topic whatsoever. The reply you receive should be on

Above: Illinois, Pennsylvania, New York, and Massachusetts state seals.

state letterhead, which will include an official seal of the state. Similarly, you could write to a city or even the federal government and expect the response to include a free sample of their seal. If you don't know what to write about, try this:

Dear Sir or Madam:
As a citizen of [name your city, state, or country], I am interested in knowing more about our [city, state, or country] seal. Could you please provide me with an example of our seal and direct me to the proper department where I may further inquire as to the history of its design.

Sincerely,

Mack Thuniphe

This letter will get you more information than you will ever need about the official seal of any jurisdiction you desire.

You can then photocopy the seal and alter it with white-out to make it your own. Or, you can scan it into your computer (my favorite) and use a paint program to alter it. You could also photocopy/scan two or more official seals and make a hybrid.

If you're artistically inclined, you could always refer to the other seals as examples and make your own either freehand or with the help of a PC painting program.

For the completion of our "no frills" example, all you need to do is make or find an official seal and paste it to the transparency master at the location indicated by our cross hairs.

MAKING A TRANSPARENCY

Tired of all these detailed instructions? Well, here's a break. Paste your official seal to the cross hairs of a printed copy of SIG&SEAL.BMP. Photocopy the result onto a transparency sheet. You are done.

SHOOTING DOWN THE ID

It is beyond the scope of this book to teach you photography. If you are not a good photographer, an excellent reference source for the novice is Tom Grimm's book, *The Basic Book of Photography* (New York: Plume Books New American Library, 1985). This book covers everything from operating your camera to selling your work. Other chapters include choosing films, close-up photography, lighting, exposure, and photographing under special conditions.

Mr. Grimm's book (as well as other books on photography) includes a section on making copy negatives. In effect, this is what you are doing when you are shooting down the ID. You are merely taking a picture of a picture. To get the right size you will need a macro (close-up) lens.

Here are the steps:

Print out a copy of WORK_ID.BMP.
Fill out the ID with a typewriter or use VTLSTATS.WRI.
Sign at the bottom (use two different handwriting styles).
Place trimmed passport photo in upper left corner.
Place transparency sheet on top to complete assembly.
Hold everything flat and in place with a piece of glass.

Here's where a camera tripod comes in handy. Using a telephoto lens on its "macro" setting, you will take several exposures of the ID at varying f-stops. Overexposure is always better than underexposure. Make sure you have plenty of light and that no glare is present in your viewfinder. The ID assembly should take up 1/4 to 1/3 of the camera's field of view depending on how big you want the final ID to appear. To be safe, make exposures from varying distances (usually between 18 and 36 inches).

Send the film to a large developing plant so that the processing will be done by machine. This will ensure that nobody will see or care about what you are doing. In any case, what you are doing is not illegal and the processing plant is only interested in your money.

POOR MAN'S LAMINATION

Lamination can be done at print shops or stationery stores. However, the following laminating technique works surprisingly well.

When you get your pictures back from the processing plant, use a paper cutter to cut your best exposure into a perfect rectangle. Glue the reverse side of your ID card to the front and let the assembly dry. Then, use sharp fingernail clippers to round the edges.

A few layers of self-adhesive lamination sheets on both sides of the ID will work well enough to give the impression of professional lamination. Trim the lamination sheets with the paper trimmer so that there is a 1/8″ border around the ID assembly. Use the fingernail clippers again to round the corners of the lamination.

You may wish to practice on some of your poorer exposures until you get a nice technique down. Then you can use your best exposure for your finished product.

SUMMARY

In this chapter you learned one technique to produce a work ID. Concentration was focused on this specific effort in order to provide a solid understanding of the particular steps involved. Instead of a bunch of disjointed information about ID manufacture, you now have a complete process that can be expanded and built upon. After you assemble the example in this chapter, you can then see where to make alterations and customizations in designing an ID specific to your own needs. I trust that your second effort will be much better than your first. Mine was!

CHAPTER SEVEN

Banking

Considering all that we have covered so far on establishing Social Security Numbers, Employer Identification Numbers, and business entities, you may think that there is little left to be said on the subject of money. Granted, we have covered many legal aspects of handling finances, but there is more to consider beyond legalities. What of practicality? The following are some fine points that I, as a detective who has helped others disappear, have learned over the years.

PERSONAL ACCOUNTS

If all you need is a private bank account, the solution may be something as simple as using somebody else's. Once, I took over my father's bank account, complete with $1,000 in overdraft protection. He was retiring and moving to a more agreeable climate. He said, "Here you go."

At the time I was very young and had no credit, so this helped a great deal. I simply signed his name on the checks and no one was ever the wiser. Upon my father's death, I had the option of continuing to use the account (as well as several others) or closing them out so that my dad could rest in peace. I opted for the latter.

The point is, if you aren't planning on starting a new life but simply are in need of some financial privacy, there may be no need to get carried away with secret accounts, business entities, and SSNs. You just need to ask a close friend or trusted family member to open a checking account for your use.

You may wish to have your trusted friend or family member open a savings account for you instead and pay your bills by money order. Friends and family members may be more amenable to this idea because it eliminates the worry about you bouncing checks in their name and ruining their credit. Even people who trust you may prefer to be cautious.

Unless you have good reason to do so and know precisely what you are doing, there is really not a whole lot of sense in opening a personal bank account under an assumed identity. Too many SSN databases exist, and too many laws are broken in the process. Moreover, security checks are being implemented and databases are growing at an exponential rate. What's safe today may not be safe tomorrow. For these reasons, opening a business account is preferable in most circumstances.

BUSINESS ACCOUNTS

When opening a business account, the bank representative will request some or all of the following documents:

Document	Source
Corporate Resolution	Corporate Directors Meeting
EIN (also called TIN) number	IRS Form SS-4
DBA Certificate	City/Town Hall
Business Address	Mail Drop/Residence
Business Telephone	Voice Mail/Answering Service
Declaration of Trust	You recorded this at the deeds registry

The exact requirements obviously will vary depending on the type of business entity opening the account. As a general rule, the documents you drew up to make your business "official" will probably be needed to open a business bank account.

Some banks are more lax than others on these requirements. In general, smaller banks in more rural areas are less restrictive in their requirements. Also, an extremely large initial deposit will cause a lot of bank representatives to turn their head to certain omissions. This is particularly true if the representative is heavily invested in the bank or working on commission.

USING A CHECK AS ID

A wonderfully subtle form of ID when opening any type of bank account is to have a check for the initial deposit that is made out to the person or business entity opening the account. The account representative will subconsciously assume that you're legitimate. After all, why would you have a check made out to you if you weren't you?

It is even better if the check is made out to you and your business. For example, a check payable to the order of "ACME BIRDSEED & GUNPOWDER, LTD, c/o Rowe D. Runner, CEO" looks very convincing.

The check should be drafted from a well-known business in the community. A favorite trick of mine is to go shopping for commercial office space, sign a lease, and put a deposit on a property that you like. Use the same alias or business name that you will be opening your bank account with. Most state laws allow a "no fault" termination of a lease whereby the leasee can terminate the lease, usually within three days, and request his or her deposit back. This renders the lease null and void, and there is nothing the rental agent can do about it. It's the law.

Because the rental agent is a big business, the money would have already been deposited into their bank account, and they are now required by law to issue you a check in the amount of your initial deposit.

Nothing looks better when you walk into a bank than to have a big check from a large, well-known, local business written out to you or your business entity (or both)! Be aware, however, that this might raise eyebrows in a small community, where people talk. Remember to adapt to your environment. In this case, the local business should be large enough to protect your anonymity, and the check amount should be in keeping with the income and spending habits of the area.

ADVANTAGES IN TIMING

Incorporating other tenets of human psychology can further reduce the difficulty you might encounter when attempting to establish a bank account.

If you walk into a bank when it is very busy, during lunchtime, or just prior to lunch or closing time, you will most likely be dealing with individuals who have temporarily relaxed their standards. Their mind is on getting "caught up," eating lunch, going home, or whatever the case may be. During these times, they have a tendency to push things through in order to get on with their own lives that much quicker. Opening an account during periods when the bank is advertising for new accounts and/or offering incentives to their employees or customers for establishing new accounts is yet another advantage in timing available to the identity changer or privacy seeker.

ADVANTAGES IN PSYCHOLOGY

Another advantage when opening a business account is that the bank representative is used to opening up personal accounts and is so preoccupied remembering the procedure for business accounts that he or she will pay much less attention to your personal credentials. They almost assume that your personal credentials are in order if you are opening up a business account.

Also, younger clerks make more mistakes. Keep that in mind during your travels.

ENDORSING BUSINESS CHECKS

Another nice advantage of having a business account is that you will not have to throw your signature around. When you make deposits, you only need stamp the check:

For Deposit Only
ACME Birdseed, INC
ACCT# 012-34-5678

When writing checks to pay bills, you can use a rubber stamp signature. These can be made up for you at most print shops for about $15. Give the print shop a sample of "your" signature. If you are right-handed, make up a signature with your left hand. If you are left-handed, give them your best right-handed signature. Within an hour, you will receive a stamp that you can use over and over again.

To endorse checks for deposit, you can buy a rubber stamp kit and arrange the letters to say anything you want. This is good if you have several accounts. These kits also come in handy for other purposes, as you'll see in Chapter 9.

PUTTING IT ALL TOGETHER

Using the above ideas and methods in concert will give you a comfortable advantage when dealing with bank bureaucrats. You will probably not need to use all of the above tricks to establish a bank account, but it is nice to have this information at your disposal. Armed with these advantages, you can select the concepts that apply to your particular situation and arrange your visit to the bank to allow the greatest chance of success. You want to be talking to the right clerk at the right time about the right things while possessing all of the necessary documentation that may be requested. Certainly, anybody who has done their homework to this extent will not be held in question.

If any questions or suspicions do arise, simply take your

documents and your business elsewhere. You have not broken the law, and the clerk has no authority or jurisdiction over you other than to refuse to open an account. This is not a problem. There are hundreds of other banks to choose from.

CHAPTER EIGHT

Establishing Credit

‿ᐧ

Surely you have had occasion in your life to fill out a bank loan or credit card application. You probably even had a general idea of how the companies issuing the application would like you to respond. You may have even written down some little white lies in the hopes of being considered a better candidate for credit. Most folks can pretty much guess, for example, that the lending institution is more likely to issue credit to a person possessing a respectable annual salary. You've probably fudged the numbers once or twice, thinking, "Should I be doing this? Will they call my boss in the morning? Well, maybe I'll just exaggerate a little bit and hedge my bets. Why do they ask me if I have a telephone? Is that good or bad? What difference does it make if I'm married and have children? Job title? That shouldn't matter . . ."

The fact is, it all matters.

CREDIT PROFILES: WHAT CREDITORS LOOK FOR

Most creditors issue credit on a points scoring system. Every question on the application will be assigned a certain number of points depending on how it is answered. Below, I have outlined a typical points scoring system for your review. Most companies will ask you questions hoping to obtain most or all of the following information:

CATEGORY	POINTS ALLOTTED

Age Group of Applicant:

Under 25 years of age	1
26 to 45 years of age	3
46 to 64 years of age	2
65 or older	1

Residence:

Less than 1 year at current residence	0
1 to 5 years	1
5 to 10 years	2
Over 10 years	3

Less than 1 year at previous residence	0
1 to 5 years	1
Over 5 years	2

Profession:

Professional (doctor, lawyer, executive)	5
White Collar (sales, marketing, etc.)	4
Blue Collar (construction, plumbing, etc.)	3
Other	2
Self-employed	1

Time at Current Job:

Over 10 years	5
6 to 10 years	4
3 to 5 years	3
1 to 2 years	2
Less than a full year	1

CATEGORY	POINTS ALLOTTED (con't)

Family Status:

Married	1-2
Spouse employed	1-2
1 or 2 dependent children	1-2
No children	0
More than three children	0-1

Financial History and Obligations:

0 to $600 in monthly obligations	2
Over $600	1
Previous credit with this bank	4
Previous credit elsewhere	3
Checking account with this bank	2
Checking account elsewhere	1
Savings account with this bank	2
Savings account elsewhere	1
Telephone billed to applicant	2
Telephone billed to applicant's spouse	1

The loan officer will then attempt to verify the information you provided by calling the telephone numbers you listed for your employer, landlord, etc. A good score on this system would be above 20 points. An unacceptable score would be below 12 points, and 13 to 19 points puts you in the gray area.

The thing that concerns most credit applicants is the loan officer's verification of information. Here is where I have some goodies for you. Keep the following in mind:

- Credit reviewers are human and have human qualities, including laziness.
- The loan officer is very busy and has dozen of applications to get through each day.

- The loan officer is expected to write a certain number of loans each week and needs to find good credit candidates even when few people are applying for credit.
- A loan officer may very well call your present employer and be happy to see that the phone number really exists and even happier if he is directed to your voice mail. (Remember Chapters 4 and 5?) Seeing this, most loan officers will assume you did not lie about your previous employer and will not bother to check it out.
- A busy loan officer may call your landlord and, upon hearing "You've reached Sunshine Apartments . . ." check off that box on your application and award you two points.

One time, a credit reviewer left two messages for me at my "place of business" (i.e., voice mail service). The message was, "I need to speak with Mr. Sheldon Charrett to verify his employment." At the time I was very busy and had enough credit, so I never bothered to call back. Nevertheless, two weeks later I had a credit card from that company. The credit reviewer, anxious to move on, apparently decided the valid phone number and voice mailbox was sufficient proof of my employment.

BE WARY OF MAIL DROPS

Major credit bureaus are now databasing known mail drops and comparing existing and newly established credit profiles to this database.

A mail drop can be used provided you know for certain it is not part of a database. A good starting point is to purchase a book that lists all known mail drops by area and patronize an unlisted drop. There are a few of these books on the market, as mentioned earlier.

However, if the book is not current or simply not thorough, how will you know that your target mail drop is not part of some newer, more thorough database somewhere else? The truth is, you can't ever know for sure. You can benefit by avoiding such places as Mail Boxes Etc. and other well-known mail-receiving establishments. You will definitely want to avoid anything listed under "Mail Receiving Services" or any similar heading in the Yellow Pages, as this is the most likely source for the information in these databases.

The best type of place to get a mail drop is one that does not specialize in them but just happens to have a few mailboxes that you can rent. Mom-and-pop establishments are the best.

Because of the databases mentioned earlier, nothing is safe when it comes to mail drops. Any establishment that rents you a mailbox will require you to fill out a form for the post office. If the postal service ever decides to sell or trade this information, only illegal mail drops will be safe. But how long do you think an illegal mailbox will stay in operation? Not long when you consider the fact that the post office will eventually stop delivering to a mailbox that is not registered.

CREDIT BUREAUS:
THE ULTIMATE PURVEYORS OF INFORMATION

Aside from the obvious advantages of having good credit, you can also use credit bureaus to obscure your existing identity through mutations. Sometimes a gradual mutation of your own identity can be a useful means of obtaining some minor privacy. The system's immense desire for information gathering renders it susceptible to the creative imagination of the identity changer.

I will use my own name and show how it has mutated over the years. The major credit bureaus have credit profiles on at least three of these mutations.

My name is Sheldon X. Charrett IV. When I was little, my parents called me Shelly, and as I got older people started calling me Shell (partly because of my name and partly because I didn't talk much). Of course, my teachers always called me Sheldon. Due to these quite innocent reasons, I have at various times been known as Sheldon X. Charrett IV, Sheldon X. Charrett Jr., Shelly Charrett, Shell Charrett, Shell X. Charrett, and Sheldon "Shell" Charrett.

Now add the mutations caused by error of various mailing

list compilers and greedy credit card companies anxious to get me on their lists: Sheldon X. Charrette, Sheldon X. Charelle, Sheldon Charrett V, Shell Charet, Shelly Charnette, Sally Charrett, Shell Sharette, and Shell Charretti.

For most of my life I lived at 209 Heron Street in New Rochelle, New York. But over the years I have also received mail in my name for 299 Heron Street, 29 Heron St., 20 Mount Heron St., 209 Hermon St., and 209 Harem St.

All that was needed was to add one more thing to the soup: the filing of a mail forwarding card with the U.S. Postal Service. Information hounds *love* to research mail forwarding databases! List compilers deem themselves hot tortillas because they can track people down and keep mailing lists up to date.

From there it was a relatively simple matter to exploit the system's hunger for information and become Sherri Cheri with a wonderful credit history and a valid mailing address at a mom-and-pop laundromat.

Of course you could extend this indefinitely by letting your already mutated identity continue to mutate, ramify, bifurcate, and otherwise live out the life of an amoebae, splitting into two, four, eight . . . Well, you get the picture. The possibilities are astoundingly infinite. With careful planning and some research at your state's vital statistics registry, you can control the mutations so that your name just happens to have a birth certificate associated with it. All this happened through no real fault of your own. After all, is it up to you to quell the modern flow of information? Heck, all you wanted was a private mailbox and now you're someone else!

FINAL NOTES ON CREDIT

Credit grantors and credit bureaus are fairly powerful entities. As with any powerful adversary, the best approach is to use their power against them. They are big and bureaucratic and, therefore, fallible. There is no need to try and beat the credit bureaus at their game. The trick is to use their own game against them.

CHAPTER NINE

PI Tricks and Tips

⌣•

When you make your living watching people who don't know they're being watched, it's hard not to learn a thing or two about the inner workings of the human mind. You also pick up a lot of tricks along the way that may or may not be interrelated—depending on your world perspective, that is. I tend to believe that, sooner or later, everything is connected to everything else. Eventually, somebody, somewhere, somehow, in some way is going to use the words "haiku" and "tuna fish sandwich" in the same sentence. See?

What follows are some comments, ideas, tips, tricks, and suggestions that find commonality in the life of an identity changer.

PART ONE:
THE REALM OF THE TERMINALLY PARANOID

So you've done it. You're sitting in your new home, which is rented or titled to some person who doesn't really exist. You can no longer contact your family or friends. Boredom sets in. Your mind begins to wander as the Talking Heads are singing in the background, *"This is not my beautiful house, this is not my beautiful wife!"* You begin to wonder if the neighbors buy your story, if the landlord has contacted the FBI, if the lady down the hall is working undercover!

THE MODERN IDENTITY CHANGER

Just relax. This is only natural.

You've upset your whole lifestyle, your whole existence, and on top of that, you are in no position to "call up the guys" to go out and forget about life for a while.

There are plenty of things you can do to help yourself relax, regain control over your life, and alleviate the paranoia that may be setting in. If you believe that the lady down the hall is spying on you, then next time you see her, have a talk with her. You will know after a few minutes of casual conversation who she really is, and this will be one less thing for you to worry about. And what about that landlord? Well, his only concern is the rent, right? After all, he's not going to risk a vacancy by getting you thrown into a federal penitentiary. So, just pay your rent on time!

Besides, you'll never see the spies if they're any good at what they do. It's when you *don't* see spies—then you can get nervous.

Oops. I suppose that doesn't make you feel any better. Although I'm joking, there is an element of truth to what I say. If you think you spy a spy, you probably don't.

The best way to gain confidence in your new surroundings is to achieve a better understanding of those surroundings. The way to rid yourself of the spy-demons that lurk in the shadows is to give them a taste of their own medicine. The best defense is a good offense. We can skirt the issue by using old clichés all night, but when it comes down to brass tacks, we're talking about spying back.

You will feel a tremendous amount of relief when you find out that the neighbors could care less about you. They are wrapped up in their own living, loving, and perhaps even some sociopathic activity of their own.

If you want to gather intelligence on your neighbors, two great resources are cordless phones and cellular phones. Many of your neighbors will have one or both of these marvels of modern technology, and the signals from both can be picked up on a handheld scanner. Thanks to the ECPA (Electronic Com-

116

munications Privacy Act) of 1986, newer scanners won't receive cellular signals. You may want to search the used market for older scanners, which are either cellular capable or can be modified to become cellular capable.

Thanks also to the ECPA of 1986, the interception and monitoring of cellular telephone frequencies is illegal. Therefore you would only be purchasing or modifying a cellular-capable receiver in anticipation of the reversal of this insane law, right? Because as long as this law is in effect, you will be breaking it and subject to fines and/or imprisonment if you listen to cellular telephone conversations.

Conversely, there is currently no federal law prohibiting the interception and monitoring of cordless telephone conversations. However, various states and local districts, most notably California, have passed laws prohibiting the interception of any electronically transmitted signal. Therefore, you will need to check applicable state laws before intercepting any electronically transmitted communications. I trust that you will.

If you are not electronically literate, there are a few companies out there that specialize in the modification of cellular-capable receivers. Search out such companies on the World Wide Web.

While you're at it, you may also want to invest in a DTMF decoder. These little gadgets will decode any Touch-Tone phone beeps that happen to come in over your scanner. Companies that sell these can also be found out on the World Wide Web using such keywords as "DTMF," "Scanner," and "Modification." If you're not on-line, a letter to each of these companies should get the ball rolling for you:

BNK
P.O. Box 1151
Andover, MA 01810

BNK makes a great DTMF decoder with a 16-character LCD readout. The model accepts input from a scanner, tape recorder, or telephone line and will hold the decoded tones in memory, even if the power is turned off.

BNK will also do scanner modifications *if* your request is very specific. If you send them a letter asking if a certain scanner can be modified, you will probably not get a response. However, if you say, "I have a Radio Shack PRO-2004, and I would like to modify it to receive the 800 Mhz band," you will probably receive a quote in the mail.

> California Grapevine Communications
> 23362 Peralta, Suite 1
> Laguna Hills, CA 92653

These guys have all sorts of cellular-type gadgets that you might wish to check out. Their stuff is more sophisticated, however. A nice product that they carry is their cellular phone "extension."

Since you now have a scanner, you might as well program in all of the local police frequencies so you can keep tabs on those guys too. If you don't know the police frequencies for your particular area, a good reference book is the *Betty Bearcat Frequency Directory*. For the most accurate frequencies, be sure to get the most recent edition for your region. The book is published by the Indianapolis-based Uniden Corporation of America and can be found in most any store that sells scanners.

NERVOUS ABOUT YOUR MAIL? TIME FOR SOME TEA!

Sooner or later you will receive a piece of mail that looks like it could be from a lawyer, bill collector, the IRS, jury duty, etc. If so, don't worry. Put the flame under the kettle and have a cup of tea!

It would be nice to find out the contents of the envelope without opening it, wouldn't it? That way, if you don't like the contents or if they seem to show that someone is on your trail, you can send the envelope back stamped "Addressee

Unknown," "Addressee Moved," or whatever to throw them off your trail.

Obviously, you can't find out the contents without opening the envelope, so you'll have to do the next best thing: steam it open. Perhaps you've tried this before and became frustrated, thinking that steaming open mail was only something that television characters could do.

Fret not. It can be done, and done well. If you use the following procedure, you will have the envelope open in less than a minute without damaging the flap. In fact, the flap will still have enough good "glue" to seal the envelope back up without anybody ever knowing. Here is the procedure.

Get a metal letter opener or a knife. By now the kettle should be boiling and whistling away. Shut off the flame. Clean the top of the kettle's spout with a damp dishcloth so that no dirt, grease, or grime is transferred onto the envelope.

Hold the envelope over the spout flap-side down so that the steam is evaporating right onto the lip of the flap and place your letter opener or knife into the flap. Gently slide it across the now-moist glue in a slight sawing motion. If done right, it should glide smoothly across the flap while opening it. *Do not* use any force, and do not leave the steam in any one area for too long or you'll melt away all the glue.

Remove the contents of the envelope, noting the exact arrangement of the enclosed materials so you can put everything back the same way (address must show through window if there is a window). If you find that someone is on your trail, stuff the letter back into the envelope and stamp the envelope "Addressee Unknown." Be sure to not use your handwriting when you do this. One of those rubber stamp kits we discussed in Chapter 7 are handy for stamping envelopes as well as endorsing business checks.

Drop the envelope in a mailbox in a different city or town so your local post office and mail carrier will not be confused by your denial of being at that address.

• ⤳

RESISTING TEMPTATIONS

A trick often used by bill collectors, investigators, and other nasty nosies is the old "send the sucker a check" routine. The routine works like this.

The investigator or bill collector, unable to find out where a particular subject does his or her banking, will send the subject a check made out by a bogus business entity. (Yes, they use them too!) A subject who is not street smart may be tempted to deposit the check into his or her bank account. *Big mistake!* When the investigator gets the check back, it will have been stamped by your bank when it was cleared. Bingo! The investigator now knows where he can attach assets and also has a better idea of where you are truly hanging out these days.

The best choice is to throw the check away. Some unscrupulous people I have known have "lost" these checks in poor neighborhoods so that they could be fraudulently cashed by homeless people or drug addicts, further throwing the investigator off the trail. Doing this, however, may be construed as assisting in a felony and could amount to another charge against you.

If you really want to cash the check, take it to the bank on which it is drawn. This really annoys investigators, as it causes them to lose money without gaining any additional information about their subject.

SAFE DRIVING METHODS FOR THE TERMINALLY PARANOID

At red lights and stop signs, keep a car-length between your front bumper and the vehicle in front of you. Be prepared to turn out to the left or right if someone comes running toward you with a flamethrower. Always have an escape route in mind.

Always know who is behind you on the highway or back roads. Pay attention to their movements. Are they trying too hard to stay a certain distance behind you? Do they appear to be talking to themselves? (If so, they may be speaking to their surveillance partner by radio.)

If you suspect you are being followed, use the following tactics to find out:

- Take three right turns. If the car you were suspicious of is still behind you, you are probably being followed.
- Go around a rotary twice. Again, if your tagalong made the same "mistake" you did, you are probably being followed.
- Pull over or go to a store. If the suspected vehicle also makes a pit stop, see what happens when you start driving again. If the other driver abruptly resumes his "trip," you are probably being followed.

If you determine that you are in fact being followed, executing any of the following ideas will help temporarily throw someone off your trail:

- Drive right by your exit, street, apartment complex, or house (whichever applies).
- Go somewhere you never went before and act as if it's very important that you are there. Let your follower take a bunch of meaningless notes.
- Go "home" for the night to a motel. Pay the clerk and slip out the back. Return for your vehicle when the PI leaves.

Never drive while intoxicated. When you are driving, you are vulnerable. If you are drunk, you will eventually get cocky and make a mistake. Don't do it.

Let tailgaters pass you when it is appropriate to do so. This keeps you in the middle of the traffic stream, where you will stand out less to the authorities. Also, the speeders will keep the police busy if there should be any on the road ahead.

Conversely, if there is some reason you do not want a police car directly behind you, you may wish to keep the tailgater where he is. This way, when a police cruiser cuts out into traffic, he will be behind the tailgater instead of you.

Always register your vehicles to a mail drop in a company name (trust, corporation, etc.). By doing so, it will not lead somebody to your front door if they ever run your license plate.

PART TWO: DEALING WITH PAST CREDITORS

In the off-chance that your reason for establishing a new identity is to avoid past creditors (gee, who would do a thing like that?), I will share with you some basic commandments that have helped my clients over the years. Although presented in the context of creditor evasion, these commandments are also invaluable in other identity changing endeavors.

KNOW THINE ENEMY

Creditors are like homing pigeons. If you have good credit, they will seek you out and solicit you perpetually until you apply for their "preapproved" credit card or take out a loan from their bank. After that, they'll solicit you just for the sake of soliciting you. Then, if you get stuck and can't pay, they will hound you until you fork over some cash that you probably don't have or have to get from another creditor.

But also know this: banks and credit card companies are businesses, and business is all numbers. Creditors enter into all loans knowing full well that a certain percentage of these loans, usually four to five percent, will never be paid back. Thus, our creditor friends set up special departments or subsidiary corporations to deal with this four to five percent while the rest of the company happily goes about its business, raking in more money than you'll ever be able to imagine.

These "collectors," as they are called, then endeavor to "recapture" some of the creditor's losses. They do this by calling up clients who have been unable to pay and encouraging them to make payments on their debt.

Any given bill collector sits behind a desk for eight hours a day making phone calls. They go right down their list making call after boring call. Some of the people they call are scared or feel guilty about their debt, and this makes the bill collector happy. He plays on this fear and guilt and gets the debtor to pay a portion of what they owe. The bill collector, in turn, is awarded a commission or other sales incentive as a result.

On the other hand, a small percentage of the people that the collector calls never answer their phone or, if they do, are not scared or intimidated, nor do they feel guilty. Now tell me, is the collector going to spend a lot of time on these folks? Why should he? Every list of 100 debtors he receives has between 80 and 90 people on it who are "willing to deal" with him. He gets paid for getting money out of them. Do you honestly think he's going to waste time on the 10 or 20 folks who are obviously not interested in his services? *It's a numbers game!* So, a subcommandment here is: Thou Shalt Have An Answering Machine And Screen All Calls. If and when a creditor does catch you picking up the phone, under no circumstances should you indicate that you are even remotely willing to deal with him.

Of course, it is important to remember not to challenge or taunt the bill collector. If you make the situation personal, he may become motivated to make your life miserable. If you are caught picking up the phone, be professional and courteous. If it becomes necessary to hang up on the collector, do so as professionally as possible, without sarcasm or malice.

THOU SHALT NOT FILL OUT FORMS

Credit databases are intensely updated from various sources. It is vital that you understand that *any* form you file, check you sign, application you fill out, or magazine you subscribe to will lead creditors right to your door. This is true whether they want to lend you money or collect it from you.

Most people know that the information they fill out on any credit application will eventually end up in a computer. Fewer people know that these same computer databases are updated via mail forwarding and voter registration records. Very few people realize

123

they are tracked through magazine subscriptions. Now that you are privy to this, you should conduct your affairs accordingly.

THOU SHALT BRAZENLY DEFEND THY RIGHTS

No matter how much you owe or what you did to get that far in debt, a bill collector must not invade your rights. Any time you feel your rights have been violated by a bill collector, write a letter to his superiors. If possible, cite the law that the bill collector has broken.

When the collection agency learns that you do not respond to phone calls and letters except to defend your rights, they will conclude that you are a bad risk. Not only will they never get anything out of you, but because you are educated and stand up for yourself, they expose themselves to liability by calling you. For a business, this is an untenable position.

Again, remember to maintain a firm, confident, businesslike manner. Engaging in a personal battle with a collector only opens the door to petty bureaucratic mischief—or worse. Your whole goal is to attract as little attention to yourself as possible.

SUMMARY

If you are scared, you are powerless. If you are always wondering when they are going to come and get you, your soul will wither away and your life of freedom will be meaningless.

By taking action and making the first move, you are placing yourself in a position of power and control. This is a much nicer way to live. Let the nasty nosies and the past creditors and investigators chase the scared and the guilt-ridden. By believing in yourself, protecting your rights, and staying alert, you can ward off the jackals that would otherwise come crawling. Let them chase those who roll over and play dead. You are too intelligent for their game.

CHAPTER TEN

Going Home

If you pull the big Houdini, you have to consider the possibility that one day you may wish to return home. Strictly speaking, if you're thinking about going home before you have even left, maybe you are not ready for this trip.

"Yeah, yeah, okay mom . . ." I hear you saying, but, hey, this is reality. Think about it for a minute. Think back to all the other times you've left your home, either to go to school, take a trip, relocate for employment, or whatever. Is this any different? Well, yes. All those other times, you knew where your true home was and that you could go back anytime. But if you disappear and leave your whole life behind without so much as a word to your family and friends, there's a lot of finality.

This chapter highlights some of the more critical points of a complete disappearance.

WILL YOU BE DECLARED DEAD?

Most states have a statute where a person can be declared dead if no contact is made with that person after a specified period of time, say, seven years. In most cases, the spouse or immediate family must petition probate court in order for this to happen, as the courts will usually not act alone unless you owe the state money. If you have debts to the state and the state discovers abandoned assets belonging to you, it may petition probate court to declare you dead and have a public administrator settle your estate.

Other people to whom you are in debt may have you declared dead and proceed with action against your estate. This usually does not happen, as creditors often have no way of knowing your whereabouts unless the creditor was previously an acquaintance or knew your spouse or immediate family. In most cases, the creditor will assume you are hiding out in order to ditch your debts.

ABANDONED PROPERTY LAWS

Every state has a special office set up to handle unclaimed and abandoned property. This office is usually a division of either the state treasurer's office, the state comptroller's office, or the office of the receiver general. These are really three different terms that mean the same thing. The name of the division that handles unclaimed and abandoned property is usually the Abandoned Property Division or the Unclaimed Property Division.

All individuals residing in the state who have abandoned property on their books must turn the property over to the state for "safekeeping" within a certain statutory period. In most states, the owner of abandoned property can claim it at any time. Certain states, most notably New Hampshire, place limits on the length of time that the true owner can assert his claim. Thus, you will serve yourself well to check the applicable state law.

Knowing this, you now have two things to think about:

• Protecting assets of a past identity
• Using the treasurer's office to hide money

The obvious solution to protecting assets of a past identity is not to leave any. Sometimes this may be unavoidable or undesirable, depending on your reasons for changing your identity. If for some reason you do have assets belonging to an identity that is on the lam, you may be able to just let those assets sit for years and years. The state may eventually take possession of them but, barring any laws to the contrary, you may someday be able to retrieve those assets, with interest.

When could you claim your abandoned assets? Well, if you are only disappearing temporarily, you can claim them upon your return "home." If you've changed your identity to hide from your family and the law is not after you, you can claim these assets at some point in the future and your family will never know about it.

If you've disappeared and are hiding from the law, you may have to give these assets up for good. If you're brazen enough, wait out the statute of limitations and then go back home to establish a claim. Provided you have properly researched the statute of limitations for whatever crime you've committed in the jurisdiction in which you committed it, you are safe. Make sure, however, that there is no other minor charge associated with the crime you committed that has a longer statute of limitations. If this is the case, the state or the feds will press that charge, and a judge will give you the maximum penalty even though the other crime was "forgotten."

For example, some states set a limiting statute of seven years for armed robbery. However, the federal statute for bank fraud is 10 years. So if bank robbery is your hobby, don't assume that you are off the hook after eight years. A good prosecutor will argue that robbing a bank amounts to bank fraud, and the judge will send you away to nail you for the actual crime of armed robbery. Even though such a decision would probably get overturned in a higher court, you will be in jail for two to three years awaiting that trial.

The other useful thing about abandoned property laws is that you can use them backwards to hide money from creditors. Creditors never bother to think that their debtors may have abandoned property waiting for them, even if the creditor has a judgment against them. State departments of abandoned property do not bother to check for existing judgments prior to disbursing abandoned property proceeds.

If your state does not have a time limit (or if the time limit is long enough for your needs), the neat trick here is to have one of your "businesses" call the compliance division of the treasurer's office and request the form necessary for reporting abandoned property. Once you receive this form, fill it out, stating that the business has a $10,000 (or whatever) account payable to either yourself or some other business entity of which you have complete control. Send this form to the treasurer's office. A short time after this, the treasurer's office will write you stating that your business must send them a $10,000 check in order to establish an abandoned account for the person to whom the business is in debt (you). Send off the check. The treasurer's office will baby-sit your money for you while your creditors perform asset searches in bank account and real property databases. Many states will even pay interest on this money!

THE PRO AND CONS OF GOING ALONG WITH THE SYSTEM

There are those who read books such as this one in the hopes of avoiding civil or criminal prosecution. For example, clients have come to me looking to disappear in order to avoid a big lawsuit that had recently been slapped on them or to avoid an impending jail sentence.

In many such cases, it may be to your advantage to "go home," or never disappear in the first place. Of course, this depends on exactly who you've pissed off. If the impending matter is a civil lawsuit, you are probably better off seeing it through to the end. The worst thing that can happen in a civil suit is that you get a judgment against you. You will not be hauled off to jail that day. In fact, you will never be hauled off to jail as long as you do what the court says. The judge will not force you to pay more than you can afford.

In any case, if you see the civil matter through to the end, you will at least know what you're leaving behind should you decide to start a new life. Usually, civil lawsuits, even those involving fraud, can be settled through the courts and bankruptcy proceedings.

If you are expecting to be sued, then you will want to go to the library and study up on bankruptcy prior to any attempt to hide or transfer your assets. There are several good books on the subject of dealing with creditors and surviving bankruptcy. In fact, I've read so many good books on the subject that it would be unfair to list only a few here. Go to the library. They are there.

Even if you are thinking about running away from a criminal proceeding against you, you may still be better off going along with the system. Things to consider:

- Offense committed
- Evidence against you
- State that is prosecuting you
- Plea bargains available
- Actual jail time you can expect to serve

Prison is not everything people say. If it were, you would not have so many repeat offenders. Prison systems are simply another institution run by the state. They are overcrowded and as a result, most states have active work release, furlough, and house-arrest prison plans for nonviolent offenders. If you are not guilty of any violent offense, you will not be placed in the company of violent offenders, and you will probably not even see a prison that looks anything like what you've seen on television or in the movies. It will probably look more like a hospital.

On the other hand, offenses such as first-degree murder, rape, and armed robbery are taken very seriously. People guilty of any of these offenses deserve to go to prison. The emotional scars left on the victims and the victims' families are irreparable. If such offenders are convicted, they will most likely be sent to a maximum security prison, more like what is portrayed on television.

CRIMES THAT GET LIGHTER SENTENCES

Believe it or not, even charges as serious as second-degree murder are often reduced to manslaughter charges. Second-degree murder is a murder that is committed without any forethought or conspiracy, usually as the result of an escalated situation of violence whereby the offending party overreacts or acts out of passion. Courts typically recognize that humans may react by instinct in these situations and are usually sympathetic. In densely populated states, sentencing is surprisingly light, and actual jail time served is usually just enough to earn the offender a college degree.

Financial crimes against banks and credit card companies are almost never prosecuted unless unusually large amounts of money are involved. The temptation of money is just too great. Banks are expected to reduce the temptation of fraud, and courts are typically not pleased with banks that leave themselves wide open to financial crimes. The courts and prisons are simply too busy with violent offenders to waste a lot of time on credit crooks. Even when prosecuted, sentences are usually suspended or, at most, extremely light.

Financial crimes against the elderly or otherwise unwitting investors are taken more seriously, and sentencing is more harsh. Many sentences, though greater, are still suspended. However, repeat offenders will usually do jail time.

SUMMARY

This chapter has highlighted some of the serious legal issues pertaining to an identity changer's return home. Obviously, anybody considering a complete identity change has issues to consider other than the legal implications mentioned in this chapter. Separating yourself from the emotional attachments you may have with your family and community is probably the biggest issue an identity changer has to consider. However, such personal and individual topics are not suitable for a "how to" book on changing your identity. Private issues such as whether or not a person can emotionally handle their own disappearance must be left to the individual considering such serious measures.

Conclusion

Identity documents are the tools of tyranny. Big Brother's ability to control our movements, track our whereabouts, and mold our habits allows for the production of die-cast citizens and the destruction of the individual.

When the masses allow their Social Security Numbers to be used as national identifiers, the bureaucratic machine is primed. When Corporate America keeps its employees close with rudimentary health care coverage and parsimonious pension plans, the gears of the machine are greased. When people preoccupy themselves with choosing between Coke and Pepsi, Burger King and McDonalds, or Bush and Clinton, the machine is cranked and revving in high gear.

And thus the machine runs on.

But for every Winston Smith in the world who does not wish to become "6079 Smith W," there is a solution. Throw sand in the gears of that machine. Drain its grease and clog its fuel lines whenever possible. When you feel as though you've given more than enough and your privacy is on the line, run that machine in reverse for awhile. Use it against itself. For you have one great advantage over the bureaucratic machine:

You can think.

And I suggest you do.

Social Security Number Area of Issue

Alaska	574
Alabama	416-424
Arizona	526-527, 600-601
Arkansas	429-432
California	602-626
California	545-573
Colorado	521-524
Connecticut	040-049
Delaware	221-222
Florida	589-595
Florida	261-267
Georgia	252-260
Guam, Samoa, Philippines	586-587
Hawaii	575-576
Idaho	518-519
Illinois	318-361
Indiana	303-317
Iowa	478-485
Kansas	509-515
Kentucky	400-407
Louisiana	433-439
Maine	004-007
Maryland	212-220

Massachusetts	010-034
Michigan	362-386
Minnesota	468-477
Mississippi	587-588 (new issue)
Mississippi	425-428
Missouri	486-500
Montana	516-517
Nebraska	505-508
Nevada	530
New Hampshire	001-003
New Jersey	135-158
New Mexico	525, 585
New Mexico	585
New York	050-134
North Carolina	232, 237-246
North Dakota	501-502
Ohio	268-302
Oklahoma	440-448
Oregon	540-544
Pennsylvania	159-211
Puerto Rico	580-584
Railroad Board	700-729
Rhode Island	035-039
South Carolina	247-251
South Dakota	503-504
Tennessee	408-415
Texas	449-467
Utah	528-529
Vermont	008-009
Virgin Islands	580
Virginia	223-231
Washington	531-539
Washington D.C.	577-579
West Virginia	232-236
Wisconsin	387-399
Wyoming	520

Compiled from various sources.

APPENDIX B

Highest SSN Groups Issued

001	86	170	74	339	88	508	31
002	86	171	74	340	88	509	08
003	84	172	74	341	88	511	08
004	94	173	74	343	88	512	08
005	94	175	74	344	88	513	08
007	92	176	74	345	88	514	08
008	78	177	74	346	88	515	08
009	78	178	74	347	88	517	25
010	76	179	74	349	88	518	43
011	76	181	74	350	88	519	43
013	76	182	74	351	88	520	31
014	76	183	74	352	88	521	91
015	76	184	74	353	88	523	89
016	76	185	74	355	88	524	89
017	76	187	74	356	88	525	89
019	76	188	74	357	88	526	99
020	76	189	74	358	86	527	99
021	76	190	74	359	86	529	99
022	76	191	74	361	86	530	75
023	76	193	72	362	17	531	75
025	76	194	72	363	17	532	29
026	76	195	72	364	15	533	29
027	76	196	72	365	15	535	29
028	76	197	72	367	15	536	27
029	76	199	72	368	15	537	27
031	76	200	72	369	15	538	27
032	76	201	72	370	15	539	27
033	76	202	72	371	15	541	41
034	74	203	72	373	15	542	41
035	62	205	72	374	15	543	41
037	62	206	72	375	15	544	41
038	62	207	72	376	15	545	99
039	60	208	72	377	15	547	99
040	92	209	72	379	15	548	99
041	92	211	72	380	15	549	99

043	90	212	39	381	15	550	99
044	90	213	39	382	15	551	99
045	90	214	39	383	15	553	99
046	90	215	39	385	15	554	99
047	90	217	39	386	15	555	99
049	90	218	39	387	15	556	99
050	82	219	39	388	11	557	99
051	82	220	37	389	11	559	99
052	82	221	84	391	11	560	99
053	82	223	69	392	11	561	99
055	82	224	69	393	11	562	99
056	82	225	67	394	11	563	99
057	82	226	67	395	11	565	99
058	82	227	67	397	11	566	99
059	82	229	67	398	11	567	99
061	82	230	67	399	11	568	99
062	82	231	67	400	45	569	99
063	82	232	41	401	45	571	99
064	82	233	41	403	45	572	99
065	82	235	39	404	45	573	99
067	82	236	39	405	45	574	13
068	82	237	77	406	45	575	65
069	82	238	77	407	45	577	25
070	82	239	77	409	73	578	23
071	82	241	75	410	73	579	23
073	82	242	75	411	73	580	29
074	82	243	75	412	73	581	99
075	82	244	75	413	73	583	99
076	82	245	75	415	73	584	99
077	82	247	93	416	41	585	99
079	82	248	93	417	41	586	17
080	82	249	91	418	41	587	75
081	82	250	91	419	41	590	35
082	80	251	91	421	41	591	35
083	80	253	87	422	39	592	35
085	80	254	87	423	39	593	35
086	80	255	87	424	39	594	35
087	80	256	87	425	75	596	40
088	80	257	87	427	75	597	40
089	80	259	87	428	75	598	40
091	80	260	85	429	75	599	38
092	80	261	99	430	85	600	35
093	80	262	99	431	85	602	68
094	80	263	99	433	87	603	68
095	80	265	99	434	87	604	68

097	80	266	99	435	87	605	68
098	80	267	99	436	87	606	68
099	80	268	96	437	87	608	68
100	80	269	96	439	85	609	68
101	80	271	96	440	04	610	68
103	80	272	96	441	04	611	68
104	80	273	96	442	04	612	68
105	80	274	96	443	04	614	68
106	80	275	96	445	04	615	68
107	80	277	96	446	04	616	68
109	80	278	96	447	04	617	68
110	80	279	96	448	02	618	68
111	80	280	96	449	99	620	68
112	80	281	96	451	99	621	68
113	80	283	96	452	99	622	68
115	80	284	96	453	99	623	66
116	80	285	94	454	99	624	66
117	80	286	94	455	99	626	66
118	80	287	94	457	99	627	38
119	80	289	94	458	99	628	38
121	80	290	94	459	99	629	38
122	80	291	94	460	99	630	38
123	80	292	94	461	99	632	38
124	80	293	94	463	99	633	38
125	80	295	94	464	99	634	38
127	80	296	94	465	99	635	38
128	80	297	94	466	99	636	38
129	80	298	94	467	99	638	36
130	80	299	94	469	27	639	36
131	80	301	94	470	27	640	36
133	80	302	94	471	27	641	36
134	80	303	13	472	27	642	36
135	94	304	13	473	25	644	36
136	94	305	13	475	25	645	36
137	94	307	13	476	25	646	18
139	94	308	13	477	25	647	16
140	94	309	13	478	23	648	01
141	94	310	13	479	21	701	18
142	94	311	13	481	21	702	18
143	94	313	13	482	21	703	18
145	94	314	13	483	21	704	18
146	94	315	13	484	21	705	18
147	94	316	13	485	21	707	18
148	94	317	11	487	08	708	18
149	94	319	88	488	08	709	18

139

151	94	320	88	489	08	710	18
152	94	321	88	490	08	711	18
153	94	322	88	491	08	713	18
154	94	323	88	493	08	714	18
155	94	325	88	494	06	715	18
157	92	326	88	495	06	716	18
158	92	327	88	496	06	717	18
159	74	328	88	497	06	719	18
160	74	329	88	499	06	720	18
161	74	331	88	500	06	721	18
163	74	332	88	501	06	722	18
164	74	333	88	502	19	723	18
165	74	334	88	503	23	725	18
166	74	335	88	505	33	726	18
167	74	337	88	506	31	727	10
169	74	338	88	507	31	728	14

As of January 1st, 1993

USC Title 18, Section 1028: Fraud and Related Activity in Connection with Identification Documents

In order to dance around the law, you must first know it. You will also want to know what you are getting into if you decide to break the law completely. What follows is the complete text of the False Identification Crime Control Act of 1982, a/k/a Public Law 97-398. No book on the subject of identity changing or identity documents could possibly be complete without it. Now that you have a copy of this very important section of the United States Code, do yourself a favor and become familiar with it. Know what you are getting into!

Public Law 97-398-DEC. 31, 1982   96 STAT. 2009

97th Congress

An Act
To amend Title 18 of the United States Code
to provide penalties for certain false identification related crimes.

*Be it enacted by the Senate and House of Representatives of the
United States of America in Congress assembled,* That this Act may
be cited as the "False Identification Crime Control Act of 1982."
    Sec. 2. Chapter 47 of title 18 of the United States code is
amended by adding at the end the following:

*Section 1028. Fraud and related activity in connection with identi-
fication documents*

(a)   Whoever, in a circumstance described in subsection (c) of this
section
     (1)   knowingly and without lawful authority produces an
           identification document or a false identification document;
     (2)   knowingly transfers an identification document or a false
           identification document knowing that such document was
           stolen or produced without lawful authority;
     (3)   knowingly possesses with intent to use unlawfully or
           transfer unlawfully five or more identification documents
           (other than those issued lawfully for the use of the
           possessor) or false identification documents;
     (4)   knowingly possesses an identification document (other
           than one issued lawfully for the use of the possessor) or a
           false identification document, with the intent such
           document be used to defraud the United States; or
     (5)   knowingly produces, transfers, or possesses a document-
           making implement with the intent such document-making
           implement will be used in the production of a false
           identification document or another document-making
           implement which will be so used;
     (6)   knowingly possesses an identification document that is or
           appears to be an identification document of the United

States which is stolen or produced without lawful authority knowing that such document was stolen or produced without such authority; or attempts to do so, shall be punished as provided in subsection (b) of this section.

(b)   The punishment for an offense under subsection (a) of this section is

(1)   a fine of not more than $25,000 or imprisonment for not more than five years, or both, if the offense is

(A)   the production or transfer of an identification document or false identification document that is or appears to be

(i)   an identification document issued by or under the authority of the United States; or

(ii)   a birth certificate, or a driver's license or personal identification card;

(B)   the production or transfer of more than five identification documents or false identification documents; or

(C)   an offense under paragraph (5) of such subsection;

(2)   a fine of not more than $15,000 or imprisonment for not more than three years, or both, if the offense is

(A)   any other production or transfer of an identification document or false identification document; or

(B)   an offense under paragraph (3) of such subsection; and

(3)   a fine of not more than $5,000 or imprisonment for not more than one year, or both, in any other case.

(c)   The circumstance referred to in subsection (a) of this section is that

(1)   the identification document or false identification document is or appears to be issued by or under the authority of the United States or the document-making implement is designed or suited for making such an identification document or false identification document;

(2)   the offense is an offense under subsection (a)(4) of this section; or

(3)   the production, transfer, or possession prohibited by this section is in or affects interstate or foreign commerce, or

143

the identification document, false identification document, or document-making implement is transported in the mail in the course of the production, transfer, or possession prohibited by this section.

(d) As used in this section
   (1) the term "identification document" means a document made or issued by or under the authority of the United States Government, a State, political subdivision of a State, a foreign government, political subdivision of a foreign government, an international governmental or an international quasi-governmental organization which, when completed with information concerning a particular individual, is of a type intended or commonly accepted for the purpose of identification of individuals;
   (2) the term "produce" includes alter, authenticate, or assemble;
   (3) the term "document-making implement" means any implement or impression specially designed or primarily used for making an identification document, a false identification document, or another document-making implement;
   (4) the term "personal identification card" means an identification document issued by a State or local government solely for the purpose of identification; and
   (5) the term "State" includes any State of the United States, the District of Columbia, the Commonwealth of Puerto Rico, and any other commonwealth, possession or territory of the United States.

(e) This section does not prohibit any lawfully authorized investigative, protective, or intelligence activity of a law enforcement agency of the United States, a State, or a political subdivision of a State, or of an intelligence agency of the United States, or any activity authorized under title V of the Organized Crime Control Act of 1970 (18 U.S.C. note prec. 3481).